THE EASY 5-INGREDIENT INDIAN COOKBOOK

THE EASY ── 5-INGREDIENT Indian COOKBOOK

75 Classic Indian Recipes Made Simple

Meena Agarwal

PHOTOGRAPHY BY MARIJA VIDAL

ROCKRIDGE
PRESS

For general information on our other products and services or to obtain technical support, please contact our Customer Care Department within the United States at (866) 744-2665, or outside the United States at (510) 253-0500.

Rockridge Press publishes its books in a variety of electronic and print formats. Some content that appears in print may not be available in electronic books, and vice versa.

Interior and Cover Designer: Stephanie Mautone
Art Producer: Alyssa Williams
Editor: Leah Zarra
Production Manager: Martin Worthington

Photography © 2022 Marija Vidal, food styling by Stéphane Réau.

Paperback ISBN: 978-1-63878-442-5
eBook ISBN: 978-1-63878-991-8
R0

To Hubby Dear and Baby Dear, my strongest cheerleaders and toughest food critics. I love you guys to bits!

Contents

Indian Cooking

Hello!

When I look back, it is clear that food brought our family together. Anytime someone had big news to share or any sort of celebration, food would become the center of our attention. I remember most of our birthdays not by the gifts we received, but by the feasts my mom prepared. Trips home from college during the summer were often preceded by telephone calls planning out the menu for the day I arrived. Most of our weekends were spent entertaining friends and family.

Food holds a very special place in any Indian household. If a couple announces that they are about to get married, the first discussion is about what menu to design. No celebration in any Indian home feels complete without a table laden with colorful dishes end to end, varying in flavor and texture. It's no surprise, then, that most Indians take immense pride in showing off their kitchens.

I inherited this passion and feel compelled to share it with others. I have been a freelance food writer and blogger, specializing in Indian food, for the last 18 years. I am a cooking instructor and recipe developer and have worked with many brands like KitchenAid, Hamilton Beach, Breville, Dairy Farmers of Canada, and Canadian Turkey. I have also written three other cookbooks. But now I want to share with you the joys, pleasures, and simplicity of Indian cooking at home.

Home Is Where the Heart Is

Of the few complaints I get about Indian cooking, the most frequent is based on the myth that Indian cooking is just too hard. Now before you roll your eyes at me and say, "Yeah sure, easy for you, you're Indian!" just hear me out. True, I was born Indian in an Indian household with a mom who cooks the most delicious Indian food I know. But truth be told, and contrary to what I would like to believe, I was not born with Indian culinary instincts in me. I, too, started off without very much knowledge. So, with the idea of "if I can do it, so can you" in mind, I encourage you to give Indian cuisine a chance. This book will prove to you just how simple, quick, and often healthy Indian food can be.

Most of us lead very busy lives, running from one commitment to another. If it's not work, then it's our family members or friends who demand our time. Although we all try to prepare wholesome meals and eat as well as we can, we can sometimes find ourselves in a rut. This book will help you dig out of that rut and re-create the wonderful and vibrant flavors and textures so present in Indian cooking, using equipment and ingredients that are easily accessible outside of India. Moreover, I strongly stand by my promise to offer you exceptional results with 5 ingredients or fewer. From tempting pakoras to hearty curries and mouthwatering stir-fries, you will be amazed at how quick and easy it can be to create a whole new world of flavor in your own kitchen.

Indian Recipes for American Tables

When you're starting out on the road to Indian cuisine, it's easy to lose yourself in the wide selection of spices. They may seem intimidating at first, but as you go along, trying things out and acquainting yourself with the robust flavors, you can't help but get excited at the prospect of shopping and stocking your spice racks with some of the unique offerings. Indian food is full of flavor, plus it can easily cater to both vegetarians and meat lovers. It is for this reason that Indian-inspired cuisine is so popular worldwide.

But to back up a bit, when it actually comes down to cooking simple Indian food, you only need to be familiar with a handful of select spices and their flavors. My recipes are inspired by classic dishes, but dressed up to suit North American tastes and tables. Although in India and in many Indian homes, a meal can take on giant proportions—with many, many dishes for many, many people—the recipes in this book are much simpler and geared to busy lives. Most are created to serve four people and can be eaten on their own or served with a bit of rice or a salad. The focus here and now is flavorful dishes rather than enormous spreads. Of course, that's not to discourage you from embarking on your own Indian feast if you're feeling ambitious.

Now it's time to get started. Chapter 1 will walk you through the basics of 5-ingredient Indian cooking.

1
Your Indian Kitchen

As a cuisine, Indian food is robust in flavors, colors, textures, heat index, and aromas. Although there certainly are recipes in Indian cooking that require a long list of ingredients and some dedicated time, so many dishes can be made quickly and with just a handful of readily available ingredients. These are the everyday recipes typical of Indian home cooking. And these are the recipes, ingredients, tools, and techniques that I will share with you in this book. This chapter offers you some background information, a quick look at Indian regional cooking and food, a primer on the staples of Indian cuisine, as well as the tools you'll need to start making these incredibly flavorful 5-ingredient recipes.

Easy Indian Cooking

When it comes to Indian food and cooking, it may seem like the only way to cook authentic Indian food is to have several pots simmering throughout the day. But cooking Indian food can be simple and easy, and the ethos of this book is that less is more. In fact, Indian cooking when it comes down to it is all about using simple, versatile, fresh, high-quality ingredients. With that in mind, you can make virtually anything using just 5 ingredients.

Traditional home-cooked Indian food is quite different from the food we find at many Indian restaurants here in North America. The focus in this book is on the relatively quick to make and simple home-style Indian food, which focuses on seasonal produce, fresh protein, and a handful of common spices and spice blends.

Here's an example. The Chicken Curry (page 74) I've shared with you in this book is way simpler and quicker to cook than any restaurant version you may find. It uses easily available and fresh ingredients rather than a laundry list of spices and the huge amounts of oil/cream used in most restaurants. Of course the advantage of cooking classic Indian dishes at home is that you can tailor the spices and flavors to you and your family's taste preferences.

The Regional Cuisines

India is a large, hugely diverse country, evident in the people and in the food. If you ever decided to travel throughout this vast subcontinent, starting from the northernmost point in the province of Kashmir and slowly descending south, making a pit stop in every major city, you would be pleasantly surprised by the variety of food you would have along the way. You'd notice the variety of spices used in the north, the heat of the food as you travel south, and the numerous variations and uses of curry in the west. A simple meal of lentils, which is one of the main staples in an Indian diet, has as many variations to it as the number of homes that cook it. The way the spices are used—more whole spices in the north and a wide range of ground spice blends in the south—and the common use of yogurt in cooking in some parts of the country as compared to the extensive use of coconut milk in others, are differences that contribute to the diversity of food available across the country.

Indian restaurants in North America tend to focus on northern and southern Indian cuisine. Butter chicken and aloo gobhi are some of the common North Indian dishes that you'll find in restaurants in North America, whereas the various kinds of dosas in restaurants come from the south. But cuisines from other regions have started to edge their way into North America in recent years, gaining some momentum. Regional Indian cuisine from Kerala, Bengal, and Gujarat have started to gain popularity. Food from these regions includes popular delicacies like spicy coconut-based curries from Kerala, classic seafood recipes from Bengal, and delicious vegetarian fare from Gujarat.

North

The northern part of India consists of states including Jammu and Kashmir, Punjab, Delhi, and Rajasthan. Northern Indian food typically revolves around a huge variety of vegetables. The climate varies drastically between the summer and winter months, and this change is reflected in the kind of food served during each season. For instance, the cold winters offer a tremendous variety of leafy greens like spinach, and other veggies like cauliflower and carrots, which are widely used during that season. North Indian cuisine is also known for its grilled delicacies like tandoori chicken, kebabs, and tikkas, and popular curries like butter chicken and dal makhana, which is a Punjabi buttery lentil dish. Some of the most common street-food delicacies—like chaat (see Crispy Potato Chaat, page 26), samosas, and chole-bhature, which is chickpea curry served on fried flatbreads—come from the north.

South

The southern part of India consists of states including Andhra Pradesh, Kerala, and Tamil Nadu. This part of the Indian subcontinent is surrounded by water, and it is for this reason that seafood plays a large part in the local diet. Because of the tropical climate, coconuts are also widely grown and often used in daily cooking. Some of the most popular South Indian food includes dosas (thin pancakes or crepes), idli (steamed cakes), Sambhar (South Indian–Style Lentil Curry, page 90), and vadas (savory fried snacks like a fritter). Being a coastal region, the south of India is also touted for its spicy fish curries. Black pepper is also grown in abundance here (hence, Pepper Chicken, page 70), and India is one of the largest exporters of this spice globally.

East

The eastern part of India consists of states including Bihar, Jharkhand, Odisha, and West Bengal. The cuisine in this region also uses a considerable amount of freshwater fish and shellfish because of its proximity to the coast, as well as a huge variety of vegetarian options. This area is widely known for its less-spicy biryani and fish curries and is also hugely popular for its street-food options like puchka (popularly known in North America as pani puri) and litti-choka, a hard dumpling made of whole wheat. Because of its particularly rainy climate, East India is known for rice cultivation and consumption.

West

West Indian food has a vast variety of vegetarian food options ranging in flavor, cooking techniques, and types of ingredients used. Many Indian states in this region are mainly vegetarian and so have developed a wide variety of plant-based options. The state of Rajasthan in northwestern India is mostly desert, so the cuisine there has developed really creative ways of using grains to compensate for the minimal availability of locally grown fresh produce. States like Maharashtra and Gujarat are well known for the multitude of beans and greens in their cuisine. Some of the most popular recipes from this region include kadhi (a thick gravy often served with pakoras), pav bhaji (a thick vegetable curry), and dhokla (steamed savory cake made of rice and lentils). The food is usually spicy, using fresh chiles. Since the climate in most of the west is hot and very dry, they rely on pickling vegetables and fruits to add robust flavors to their food.

A Few Words and Terms

You'll find many terms in Indian cooking that may be unfamiliar to you, so here is a basic primer on a few of them.

Chaat: Chaats are a kind of street food found in most parts of India and can differ in taste, texture, and style. They usually consist of a combination of something crispy, spicy, tangy, and sweet, and are topped with various spices and chutneys.

Dal: Because most people in India are vegetarians, dal (lentils), which are chockful of protein, feature prominently in Indian cuisine and are an important part of the everyday menu. Lentils can easily take on varied flavors and add richness to daily meals.

Dosa: Dosas are thin crepes from South India made mostly of a combination of rice and some kind of lentil. They are usually fried to a crisp and dunked in sambhar (a lentil soup loaded with veggies) or eaten with a side of coconut or tomato chutney.

Korma: Korma is a mild, aromatic, and creamy curry dish that has its origins in the ancient Mughlai cuisine. You can often find this served at weddings or special occasions. Its wonderful flavor comes from blending numerous spices along with a mix of nuts and cream.

Masala: This a Hindi word that means blend of spices, such as Garam Masala (page 104). Masala also refers to the blend you get after frying up onions and tomatoes with spices at the beginning of many recipes.

Naan: Unlike the simple roti, these breads are made with a yeast dough and often feature in a more elaborate meal plan. Naans are often served at weddings and special occasions where the rich food served calls for a bread with a heartier texture. Although naans are traditionally baked in a hot clay oven called a tandoor, it is quite possible to make a version of it in a regular kitchen oven.

Paneer: Paneer is a soft mild fresh cheese that is widely used in Indian cuisine. Store-bought paneer is easily available at most Indian markets or in the international aisle of a well-stocked supermarket and can be bought in large blocks. Paneer is very mild in flavor and can easily take on any flavor added to it. Because it does not melt and disintegrate at high temperatures, it is a great vegetarian option to use on the grill.

Pulao: Pulao are rice dishes that are cooked in a flavorful broth with the addition of meat, vegetables or nuts, and whole spices. A simple version of it, like the Jeera Pulao (Cumin Rice, page 96), is best served with a rich curry or a heavy lentil dish.

Roti: Rotis are traditional Indian breads made with whole wheat flour and cooked on a hot iron griddle. Unlike most breads, rotis do not include any yeast and are a regular feature at every meal. Because they have a neutral flavor, rotis pair perfectly with any curry, dal, or vegetable dish.

Samosa: Samosas are one of the most popular snacks in Indian cuisine and are commonly sold by street vendors. Traditionally, they are deep-fried and enjoyed as a snack either with a cup of tea or a side of spicy chutney in the evenings. These are bound to disappear fast, so make sure you save yourself a piece or two before handing them out.

Tikka: This often refers to grilled meats or vegetables and is by far one of the most popular dishes in Indian cuisine. A traditional tikka dish is made by threading marinated pieces of meat, paneer, or vegetables on metal skewers and cooking them in a hot tandoor oven until they are completely cooked through and charred around the edges.

Spices, Rice, and Curry

Curry is undoubtedly one of the most popular Indian dishes and can vary in style, color, and flavor within different regions throughout the country, and every household has a secret family recipe that they claim is the best! One thing to note here, however, is when I discuss "curry," I am referring to a saucey-based dish of either meat or vegetables.

Whole Spices

Spices like cumin seeds, mustard seeds, and coriander seeds are the first things added to hot oil to begin the cooking process in many dishes. Sautéing these spices helps infuse the dish with flavor as well as give it body and texture. And starting with whole spices at the beginning of the dish means the spices will continue to flavor the dish for the duration of the cooking process. It is always a good idea to bruise (break up) the spices a little before adding them to a dish, to enable maximum release of flavor. Any large whole spices (such as cinnamon sticks) are generally discarded before the dish is served. Store whole spices in individual spice jars in a cool, dry place away from direct heat. Since they generally have a strong aroma, it is best to store them separately so that the flavors remain distinct. If stored well, they can often stay fresh for a couple of months.

In traditional Indian kitchens, if a spice is to be added as a powder, the cook would start with the whole spices and then grind by hand. The spices are often dry-roasted first before being pounded to a fine powder. Buying whole spices (often in bulk) ensures that the flavors of the ground powders are always as fresh and vibrant as possible. The four classic ground spices, and some of the most commonly used spices in Indian cooking are red chili powder, turmeric, coriander, and cumin. Although these same spices may repeat in many Indian recipes, the varying proportions and methods of cooking are what can create truly distinctive flavors.

Spice Blends

Spice blends (called masalas) are a major part of what makes Indian food distinct from other Asian cuisines. These blends are the MVPs in many Indian recipes, allowing the dishes to have a minimum of ingredients yet still be layered, intricate, and wonderfully flavorful. Traditionally, these spices were freshly ground at home and then mixed together right before use to ensure freshness and maximum flavor. But today, when time is short, you can purchase fresh premade spice blends at any Indian market, online, and even in most general grocery stores. If you want to go the more traditional way and make your own, the Staples chapter (page 103) contains recipes for some of the most common spice blends. If you have trouble finding some of these spices, check out the Resources section (page 116) for brand and shopping recommendations. Here are the seasonings and masalas called for most frequently in this book:

Amchoor Powder: Amchoor is not precisely a masala, but rather a commonly used seasoning powder that adds a strong tangy flavor to food. To make amchoor, green mangos are sun-dried and then ground to a powder. You can find it at most Indian or South Asian markets. Amchoor powder is generally added to dishes that require a strong tartness in flavor (Masala Green Beans, page 56). If you can't find it, you can use fresh lemon juice instead.

Chaat Masala: Chaat masala is a salty-sour ground spice blend that is usually sprinkled on top of fresh-cut fruit or deep-fried snacks like pakoras to give them an extra edge. It mainly consists of coarse salt and amchoor powder, along with a few other spices. You get a good taste of it in Corn Chaat (Spiced Corn Salad, page 39).

Garam Masala: This robust blend of powdered spices includes cinnamon, cloves, cumin, peppercorns, bay leaves, and a few others. The color and taste in store-bought garam masala often varies depending on the kinds of spices and amounts used, but you can always makes your own; see page 104. It adds warmth to recipes like Bharwaan Baingan (Stuffed Baby Eggplants, page 48).

Panch Phoron: This traditional whole spice mix from the region of Bengal is typically used at the start of the cooking process as a tempering. The blend includes five spice seeds: mustard seeds, cumin seeds, fenugreek seeds, nigella seeds, and fennel seeds. To make your own, see page 106. This five-spice mixture imparts flavor to Patta Gobhi Ki Sabzi (Cabbage Stir-Fry, page 52).

Sambhar Masala: A traditional powdered blend from southern India, this masala is used mainly in a popular spiced lentil dish called Sambhar (South Indian–Style Lentil Curry, page 90). As with many traditional recipes, almost every South Indian home has its own special secret blend. These days you can find this spice at most grocery stores, and it can be added to pretty much anything to give it a big boost in flavor.

Tandoori Masala: This is the blend of ground spices used in most grilled Indian recipes. Though it can vary, it usually consists of ground chiles, coriander, and garam masala. It's also used in Baingan Bhaja (Fried Eggplant, page 57). To make your own, see page 105.

Rice

Historically, rice was widely grown, available, affordable, and accessible on the subcontinent. And to this day the grain is a main foundation of Indian cuisine. This filling carb serves as an excellent energy source and a lovely warm and neutral base for the varied flavors of Indian dishes.

There are many varieties of rice in the grocery store, but I personally suggest sticking to basmati rice, a flavorful long-grain rice, for Indian cooking. India is one of the leading exporters of basmati rice in the global market and it is believed to have been cultivated on the Indian subcontinent for centuries. Basmati rice gives out a slightly sweet aroma while it cooks and, when cooked properly, the grains remain separate without sticking together, so that it mixes perfectly with whatever textures and flavors you add. Indian cooks will often buy large bags—5 to 10 pounds—of basmati, but you can also find it in more manageable 2- and 3-pound amounts.

Curry

Curries, which can be a quick solution when you don't have too much time to fuss over dinner, are best enjoyed with a side of plain white rice or warm roti. You can easily whip up a quick salad and make it a complete meal.

Butter chicken, also known as Chicken Makhani at many Indian restaurants, undoubtedly has to be one of the most popular curries from the Indian cuisine. Most Indian curries vary from kitchen to kitchen, with every family swearing that they make the best one. Ingredients differ depending on the region they're from and, most important, the ingredients that grow in abundance around them. Since

STREET FOOD

India boasts numerous inexpensive, flavorful street foods that are as varied and tantalizing to the senses as the different regions where they are found. Any city you find yourself strolling through, be it Delhi or Bangalore, will tempt you with its very best offerings, street after street and stall after stall. You won't be able to keep up with the diverse tastes and textures of these Indian gems, many of which are accompanied by spicy and tangy chutneys and yogurt toppings.

Even without the delightful hawkers selling their delicacies, you can still enjoy this unique aspect of Indian culture by making your own authentic Indian street food. Some of the most popular street food recipes are in chapter 2, like the Crispy Potato Chaat (page 26), Corn Chaat (Spiced Corn Salad, page 39), and Aloo Tikki (Crispy Potato Cutlets/Cakes, page 31). These recipes are best enjoyed as part of an array of such dishes, and for a crowd, so try serving them at your next dinner party. You'll be surprised at how simple recipes with just 5 ingredients can seem so exotic and special at the same time.

meat was sometimes quite costly to serve as the main meal for a large family, people started to mix pantry staples like potatoes and seasonal vegetables into curries to stretch the recipe to feed more for less.

Smart Shopping

Before you head to the grocery store, make sure you take a quick peek at your refrigerator, freezer, and pantry to take stock of what you already have. With that in mind, create your menu plan and grocery list, then stick to it. To cut costs and shop on a budget, try to pick recipes that use overlapping ingredients, check out store circulars for sales, and cut coupons for items on the list. This will help you cut food waste and prevent those last-minute, run-to-the-store delays. Oh, and don't forget, never shop on an empty stomach!

Shopping for Fresh Produce

For Indian recipes, you will be shopping for lots of fresh produce. If you follow these tips, you'll have the best results.

◆ Shop for produce that is in season and local as much as possible. The items displayed at the front of the produce section are normally the ones in season at the moment.

◆ Store produce the way you see it stored in the grocery store. If something is refrigerated, refrigerate it.

LEFTOVERS AND STORAGE TIPS

Many Indian curries taste better the next day because the spices have that extra time to impart their flavors and infuse the dish even more. It is for this reason that many home cooks make an extra serving of a favorite recipe to enjoy another day. Plus, what a timesaver on a busy weeknight! Always make sure that the food has cooled completely to room temperature before storing it in the refrigerator. Store leftovers in airtight containers to preserve their flavors and keep them fresh.

→ I love cooking an extra batch of a pulao (rice dish) or dal (lentils) and keeping it in the refrigerator/freezer to use later. Both freeze extremely well and can be a lifesaver when you have hungry mouths to feed.

→ Bean dishes, such as Rajma (Red Kidney Bean Curry, page 91), and chanas (like Chana Masala, page 86) freeze well and often stay good for a few weeks when frozen. Store them in airtight containers in smaller portions to make it easy to thaw and reheat when needed.

→ Leftover cutlets/kebabs (such as Chicken Kebabs, page 69) taste great reheated and can easily be used as a quick, delicious filling for sandwiches and wraps.

- When an item is not in season, try the frozen section; these vegetables (and fruits) are picked and packed at their peak of freshness.

- Try buying fresh produce in a variety of different colors—eat the rainbow, as they say.

- Once home, make sure you use the produce with the shortest shelf life first (for example, eggplant will go bad more quickly than onions).

Shopping for Herbs and Spices

Fresh herbs like cilantro and mint are garnishes used a lot in Indian cooking because of their appearance and bursts of flavor. These herbs, along with fresh aromatic ingredients like ginger, garlic, and chiles, are also commonly blended with various spices to create rich and robust chutneys. Most Indian spices and spice blends are readily available at well-stocked supermarkets and online. Here are some recommendations for buying and making these items last:

- Always store fresh herbs wrapped in damp paper towels in the refrigerator to make them last longer. When choosing herbs, make sure to look for leaves that are tender and deep green in color. This indicates that the leaves are fresh and have maximum flavor.

- Dried herbs can also be used and store extremely well in the right conditions. Because they are a concentrated form of the fresh, you use a smaller amount. The rule of thumb is that you use about one-third the amount of dried as fresh.

- Store spices in airtight glass containers in a cool, dry place away from any direct heat to prevent them from losing flavor and fragrance.

- If possible, buy spices from a bulk container. This allows you to buy smaller quantities so that you can try them out and get used to their flavor without investing in large packs.

The Indian Pantry

This section will help you assemble the essential items needed to create an Indian pantry.

Keep in mind that a less expensive way to shop for many ingredients like spices and high-quality basmati rice is to buy them from the bulk bins in your local Indian market or ethnic grocery store.

Fresh and Perishable

Cilantro, Fresh: Cilantro leaves are regularly used as a garnish on Indian recipes. The leaves are tender and give out a sweet fresh aroma when chopped.

Curry Leaves: These are usually added to hot oil at the beginning of the cooking process to give a slight aromatic flavor to the dish. Curry leaves are commonly used in southern Indian cooking and can be readily found at most Indian markets.

Ginger: Fresh ginger is a pungent aromatic spice widely used in Indian cooking. It is well known and appreciated for its medicinal uses, including treating nausea, indigestion, and fighting the common cold. Ginger freezes wonderfully and you can pop any leftovers into the freezer in a sealed bag to store for a longer time. When you're ready to use it for a recipe, simply grate the ginger, skin and all, into the dish. The flavor will still be fresh and pungent, even if it has been frozen for a couple of weeks.

Mint, Fresh: Mint leaves are often used in Indian salads and curries to add a robust flavor. The leaves are also used as a garnish.

Onions: A lot of Indian recipes begin with sautéing onions to create that rich base. You can use either white, yellow, or red onions for cooking depending on what works best for you. In most cases, the choice of onion does not matter much since the spices added are often strong enough to take over. However, I recommend using red onions if possible, especially in salads and stir-fry recipes, since they add a more robust flavor to the recipe.

Potatoes: Potatoes are as popular with Indians as pasta is to Italians. You won't come across a menu of Indian delicacies without potatoes included in at least one of them. Since potatoes are quite bland on their own, they can carry the intense flavor of Indian spices really well. I generally prefer using baby yellow potatoes since they contain much less starch. However, red or white baby or fingerling potatoes also work nicely.

Spices

Coriander, Ground: Ground coriander is made by dry-roasting whole coriander seeds and finely grinding them. It deepens the flavors of curries and stir-fries.

Cumin, Ground and Seeds: Whole cumin seeds are often added to hot oil for flavoring at the start of cooking. Ground cumin adds a soft, smoky flavor while cooking. It pairs perfectly with ground coriander and they are often used together.

Mustard Seeds: The black mustard seeds used in Indian cooking differ in taste from the yellow mustard seeds used to make the condiment. Black seeds are used in Indian cooking as a tempering spice.

Red Chili Powder: Not to be confused with the seasoning blend called chili powder, this is finely ground dried red chiles. Sold in Indian markets as red chili powder, in Western markets it is more commonly known as cayenne pepper. It gives recipes a hot kick.

Spice Blends: Any or all of the spices blends described on pages 7 and 8 are good to have on hand, although making your own from scratch will have the freshest results.

Turmeric, Ground: Turmeric has always been used in Indian cooking, mostly for its medicinal and Ayurvedic properties. But take care, as a little goes a long way with turmeric; adding too much of it can give the dish a slightly bitter taste.

Canned Goods

Chickpeas: Canned chickpeas are great to have in your pantry to save time instead of soaking and cooking dried beans. Just be sure to drain and rinse them before using.

Coconut Milk: Canned coconut milk is a great addition to the pantry. It helps make rich, creamy curries. Just make sure you use full-fat canned milk, not the "beverage" sold in cartons.

Red Kidney Beans: Just as with chickpeas, canned kidney beans are great to have in your pantry as an excellent source of protein in many types of dishes.

Tamarind: Tamarind is usually used in South Indian recipes as a souring agent. Although traditional recipes call for the use of tamarind juice, you can easily use store-bought tamarind concentrate as a substitute.

Tomato Paste: Canned tomato paste is a great staple to keep in your pantry at all times. It is a simple way to add depth of flavor and texture to dishes. Once I open a can of tomato paste, I store the unused portion in the refrigerator. If you think you won't use the tomato paste up quickly, consider portioning it out and freezing it.

Dry Goods

Atta: Atta is the Indian whole wheat flour used mainly to make Indian flatbreads like Rotis (page 30) and Parathas (page 34).

Besan: Also known as chickpea flour or gram flour, besan is a gluten-free flour often used as the batter for pakoras (fritters).

Canned Tomatoes: Fresh tomatoes are generally preferred in Indian cooking, but canned tomatoes work well in curry recipes, so it's nice to keep them handy.

Lentils: Lentils are used in Indian homes on a daily basis as the protein source for many vegetarian meals. Some of the most common lentils used in everyday Indian cooking are masoor (red lentils), toor (yellow lentils), and moong (green lentils).

Rice: Basmati is the best rice to use in Indian cooking because of its lovely aroma and a texture that does not stick together (read more on page 8).

Semolina: Semolina, also known as sooji, is a form of durum wheat, and is often used for making halwa (a confection) or Chillas (Semolina Pancakes, page 25).

Chutneys and Pickles

Chile Pickle: You can find a huge variety of Indian chile pickles with a huge range of heat levels: Some are sweet, some are super-hot, and some are a combination. Or you can make your own quick and easy Instant Chile Achar (Green Chile Pickle, page 110).

Coconut Chutney: A favorite accompaniment to a spicy masala dosa, this fresh chutney is made by blending freshly grated coconut with generous amounts of green chiles, fresh ginger, curry leaves, urad dal, and mustard seeds.

Green Chutney: This fresh chutney made with mint and cilantro (see recipe, page 111) is considered by many an absolute must to accompany Indian meals. It can also do double-duty in Western meals as a pesto.

Mango Chutney: Easily found in supermarkets, this chutney is also easily made at home (see the recipe on page 112). As much as you will enjoy it with a traditional Indian meal, it also serves as a great topping for any regular sandwich.

Mango Pickle: Mango pickle is one of the most popular Indian pickles and is traditionally made with sun-dried raw mangos, cold-pressed mustard oil, and spices. The flavor, consistency, and heat level differ from region to region.

Tamarind Chutney: A slow-simmering chutney of tamarind pulp, jaggery (Indian unrefined sugar), and a mix of spices, this tangy chutney is a great dip for many Indian snacks. It is a wonderful blend of sweet and sour flavors with a hint of spice, and adds that much-needed zing to many popular street foods.

Tomato Chutney: This refreshingly sweet chutney is made by slow-cooking fresh tomatoes with curry leaves, ginger, and spices. Eaten hot or cold, it brings a wonderful boost to any simple meal. For a quick version of tomato chutney, see the recipe on page 113.

CHUTNEYS AND PICKLES

Indian cuisine stands for strong robust flavors, and there is no more apparent way to see these flavors in play than in chutneys and pickles. Most Indian meals are accompanied by both of these.

When I say pickle, these are not the classic dill pickles found in almost every kitchen in North America. Rather, an Indian pickle is a condiment (often fiery) that is used in only small amounts, much like a hot relish. Although most Indian pickles tend to be sour, you can also find a good range of sweet varieties. Mango pickle was all the rage traditionally, but now you can find pickles made with many different fruits or vegetables.

Most pickles are made by sun-drying the fruits and vegetables and then storing them in a jar of salt over a period of time. They are then mixed with oil and spices and some are then simmered for hours. It can even become a family activity, making vegetable pickle in the summer months when produce is at its freshest. Each family holds on to its own secret recipes.

Chutneys, which actually started out as a way to use leftover ingredients, can be classified into two basic categories: fresh and cooked. Fresh chutneys are intended to be eaten right away, though some will keep fairly well for a couple of days in the refrigerator. The fresh chutneys are those that are a blend of fresh ingredients and spices that require no cooking whatsoever. The cooked chutneys, however, are simmered over low heat until all of the flavors are blended well. Although there are many different types of chutney (and every Indian household has its favorite), traditionalists agree that all Indian meals require a side of tangy fresh Green Chutney (page 111).

Refrigerator and Freezer

Here are some of the essential items found in the refrigerator and freezer in most Indian homes. These are mostly used in everyday cooking and are good to have on hand in order to craft quick and wholesome meals.

Refrigerator

Fresh Produce: Indian cuisine makes extensive use of seasonal produce. Carrots, cabbage, cauliflower, eggplant, mushrooms, spinach, green beans, fresh ginger, lemons, and limes are usually the most common produce you can find in many Indian refrigerators. (This is in addition to the fresh produce stored at room temperature, of course.)

Indian Pickles and Chutneys: Indian-style pickles and chutneys come in a variety of flavors and can perk up any simple meal. Once the jar is opened, keep it in the refrigerator.

Tomato Paste: I like having canned tomato paste handy to add flavor, color, and texture to curries, so once I open the can, I store it in the refrigerator.

Yogurt: Plain yogurt is often used in curries or eaten with many Indian meals as a side dish in the form of raita (Cucumber Raita, page 108). Plain whole-milk yogurt most closely resembles the yogurt traditionally used in India, but low-fat or nonfat yogurt works equally well in many recipes. Use whatever you have on hand.

Freezer

Ginger: Fresh ginger does not have a long shelf-life, but when it's frozen it can stay fresh for months. You can store a whole piece of ginger in an airtight bag in the freezer and easily grate as much as you need.

Parathas: I often keep a good stock of frozen plain or stuffed parathas (flatbreads) to use when I'm in a pinch for time. You can easily freeze homemade ones or buy them frozen in most grocery stores. Served with some pickle/chutney and yogurt, they can make for a nice, quick meal.

Veggies: Keep an array of frozen vegetables like peas, carrots, cauliflower, and corn. These items will help you in creating quick meals by saving time on cleaning and chopping fresh produce. With a bag of frozen mixed veggies in the freezer, you will be able to cook a delicious vegetable curry or pulao (rice dish) in much less time.

Essential Equipment

Indian cooking does not require unusual utensils. For the most part, you can make do with the standard pots and pans that you may already have in your kitchen. In most cases, standard nonstick cookware will do wonderfully with most of the recipes (just be sure you are using a nonmetal utensil to avoid scratching the nonstick coating). However, if you are doing any of the recipes that require a fair amount of oil for deep-frying, make sure your pot is heavy-bottomed and deep enough so that there is at least 1½ inches of clearance from the top of the oil to the rim of the pot. Here are a few other things I believe are essential to making your time in the kitchen go as smoothly as possible.

Blender or Food Processor: You will definitely need a simple blender or mini food processor to make spice pastes and/or chutneys. You don't need anything heavy-duty, just one with sharp blades.

Cooking Tongs: It's best to opt for a pair of tongs with silicone tips that is long enough to use while sautéing as well as for use with the oven.

Heavy-Bottomed Pot: Choose one that is at least 6 to 8 quarts in capacity. This kind of pot is perfect for slow-cooking meat-based curries as well as dals and stews that would require a bit of sautéing followed by simmering. A Dutch oven that can go from stovetop cooking to a preheated oven serves this purpose well.

Instant-Read Thermometer: Using a thermometer is the best way to determine if poultry and meat are completely cooked through.

Knives: Always make sure that your knives are sharpened regularly to make chopping and slicing as easy and safe as possible. It is best to pick and choose knives that you really need, like a chef's knife, rather than investing in a full set that contains knives that you may never use.

Nonstick Saucepan with Lid: It's great to have these in two sizes: small (1-quart) and medium (3-quart). If you can only pick one, choose medium. Select one with a glass lid so that you can peek into it without lifting the lid and letting out the heat while the food cooks. Use this pan for quick-cooking curries, lentils, or vegetables that require a bit of simmer time. A nonstick coating makes this a great choice to use for cooking rice dishes like pulaos.

Nonstick Skillet: A good-quality nonstick skillet can easily substitute for the more traditional tawa (see below). A nonstick skillet is perfect to use when shallow-frying, but is also a great option to use while making Rotis (page 30) and Parathas (page 34). An 11- or 12-inch skillet is optimal for holding the amount of food in these recipes.

Rolling Pin: If you intend to make any kind of Indian flatbread, be it rotis, parathas, or puris, then a rolling pin is a must.

Not Essential, but Nice to Have

The following pieces of equipment are nice to have but not essential for the recipes in this cookbook.

Kadhai/Kadai (Round-Bottomed Pan): Traditionally, these Indian-style woks are made of thick aluminum. Using a nonstick kadhai will enable you to cut down on the amount of oil used while cooking or stir-frying. Opt for one with a glass lid.

Pressure Cooker: Pressure cookers, electric or traditional, can easily halve the cooking times of things like dried lentils and beans.

Spice Grinder: A small spice grinder is a great addition to your kitchen if you intend to make your own batches of freshly ground spice blends. Or you can use a mortar and pestle.

Tawa (Flat Griddle): A traditional tool, a tawa is a flat, heavy-duty iron pan (though you can easily use a good-quality nonstick skillet). A tawa is a great option for making rotis or any griddled Indian bread. An 11- or 12-inch tawa would work well in most kitchens.

The Core Techniques

These are some of the most common techniques used in everyday Indian home cooking. Each technique is used to impart flavor to the food, and the techniques can vary depending on the region from which the recipe originated.

Baghar (Tempering): Many Indian recipes involve a technique called tempering at the beginning or end of the cooking process. Tempering, or baghar as it is known in many parts of India, involves heating a small amount of oil with aromatics like cumin seeds, whole dried chiles, or curry leaves along with garlic, onion, or spices. The combo can be added on top of the finished dish for an extra boost of flavor.

Dum (Steaming): Many Indian curry recipes are slow-cooked using a process called dum to extract the maximum flavor from the ingredients. Dum, or steaming, is often done by covering the pan with a heavy lid and turning the heat down low, so that the food slowly cooks without letting any steam escape. This method is often used for biryani dishes.

Talna (Frying): Talna, or frying, is a technique used to add a wonderful crisp texture to dishes and is usually seen in snacks, some breads, and street food, like Puris (page 29) and Crispy Potato Chaat (Tangy Fried Potatoes, page 26).

About the Recipes

The recipes I've collected for this book were developed to be practical and easy to follow. I've tried to select recipes that represent as many cooking traditions and regions of India as possible and that are most commonly cooked in Indian homes—but without forgetting to include some restaurant favorites.

5 Ingredients

The recipes use readily available ingredients and strictly follow the 5-ingredient claim. This means that except for the standard exceptions of oil, water, salt, and pepper, every recipe in this book requires only 5 ingredients or fewer. Almost all ingredients used in the recipes can easily be found in any regular grocery store, with a handful that may require a quick trip to your nearest Indian market. However, most large retail grocery stores nowadays have a big enough international section that you will find everything you need. Although the ingredients are minimal, the recipes absolutely do not sacrifice flavor in any way.

Labels

For ease of use and to accommodate various preferences, the recipes all include labels that indicate whether a recipe is Vegan, Vegetarian, Dairy-Free, Gluten-Free, and/or Kid Friendly (in my estimation). The 30 Minutes or Less label notes when a recipe takes 30 minutes or less to make, including prep and cook time, and there are many that fit that bill.

Tips

The recipes also include the following tips:

Flavor Boost: These tips offer simple ways to enhance or change the taste, texture, or nutritional value of a recipe.

Ingredient Tip: These tips present more information on background, buying, choosing, preparing, and/or cooking a specific ingredient.

General Tip: These tips involve shortcuts or advice on how to ensure a recipe's success, or maybe a fun fact or some history about the recipe.

Substitution Tip: If an ingredient is difficult to find, or if you have a dietary concern and want to swap in a different ingredient, these tips will guide you.

Variation: This is a simple tweak that both demonstrates the versatility of a dish and gives it a different flavor profile.

Most recipes in this book are designed to feed four people. But you should feel free to adapt them to feed as many people as you need. Now it's time to get started on some Indian cooking.

Puris (Deep-Fried Indian Puffy Breads, page 29)

2
Appetizers, Breads, and Snacks

Egg Bhurji
Indian-Style Scrambled Eggs

◇◇◇◇◇◇◇◇◇◇◇◇◇◇◇◇◇◇◇◇◇◇◇

30 MINUTES OR LESS ◇ **DAIRY-FREE** ◇ **GLUTEN-FREE**
KID FRIENDLY ◇ **VEGETARIAN**

PREP TIME: 10 minutes ◇ **COOK TIME:** 10 minutes ◇ **SERVES 4**

When I was growing up, eggs featured a lot on our Sunday brunch table. However, it was hardly ever the type of fare you find at breakfast tables these days. Eggs were made to take on more distinct flavors and would always be a welcome treat. Nowadays, I find myself whipping up this recipe more often than not, and in most cases it is jazzed up to take on a new form. Egg bhurji, spiced scrambled eggs, is widely enjoyed all over India for breakfast or as a snack. I love stuffing the spicy scrambled eggs into pita pockets with some crisp lettuce and sliced cucumbers for a quick to-go lunch.

2 tablespoons canola oil

1 medium **yellow onion**, finely chopped

½ teaspoon **red chili powder**

Salt

2 medium **Roma tomatoes**, finely chopped

6 large **eggs**, beaten

Fresh cilantro leaves, finely chopped, for garnish

1. In a large nonstick skillet, heat the oil over medium-low heat. Add the onion and sauté for 1 to 2 minutes, until it is tender and lightly browned. Add the chili powder and salt to taste and cook for a few seconds. Be careful not to let it burn.

2. Add the chopped tomatoes and cook until the tomatoes soften and start to break down, 1 to 2 minutes.

3. Slowly mix in the beaten eggs and continue stirring to scramble them and incorporate them into the spices, 2 to 3 minutes.

4. Garnish with fresh cilantro and serve warm.

FLAVOR BOOST: Warm 4 flour tortillas and spread 2 to 3 tablespoons of the scrambled eggs over. Layer them with fresh lettuce, sliced tomatoes, and a tablespoon of shredded cheese. Roll the filled tortillas up tightly into wraps, and serve with Mango Chutney (page 112) on the side.

Chillas

Semolina Pancakes

◇◇◇◇◇◇◇◇◇◇◇◇◇◇◇◇◇

30 MINUTES OR LESS ◇ **DAIRY-FREE** ◇ **KID FRIENDLY** ◇ **VEGAN**

PREP TIME: 10 minutes ◇ **COOK TIME:** 30 minutes ◇ **SERVES 4**

Semolina pancakes, also known as chillas, are a favorite in northern India, traditionally served as a light evening snack with chutneys. I personally like to serve this savory snack for brunch as a switch from regular sweet flour pancakes. The semolina gives a grainy texture to the pancakes and pairs wonderfully with Green Chutney (page 111). Or serve it up with a light curry for a simple and delicious dinner. Any leftovers keep really well and are great for lunch the next day.

1 cup **semolina flour**

1 medium **yellow onion,** thinly sliced

2 tablespoons finely chopped **fresh cilantro**

½ teaspoon **red chili powder**

½ teaspoon salt

1 cup water, or as needed

2 tablespoons canola oil, for frying

1. In a large bowl, combine the semolina flour, onion, cilantro, chili powder, and salt and mix well. Slowly add the water, stirring constantly, to form a thick, pancake-like batter. Use as much water as you need to achieve this consistency.

2. In a medium nonstick pan, heat 1 teaspoon of oil over medium-low heat. Carefully ladle out 2 to 3 tablespoons of batter. Using the back of the ladle, spread it out into a thin layer (see General tip).

3. Cook the pancake for 2 to 3 minutes on each side, until it turns lightly brown and crisp along the edges. Work in batches, using more oil as needed.

GENERAL TIP: The batter won't flow easily when added to a hot pan, so do your best using the back of the ladle to spread it as much as you can without breaking it.

FLAVOR BOOST: You can definitely add some chopped green chiles to make this spicier.

Crispy Potato Chaat
Tangy Fried Potatoes

◇◇◇◇◇◇◇◇◇◇◇◇◇◇◇◇◇◇◇

DAIRY-FREE ◇ **GLUTEN-FREE**
KID FRIENDLY ◇ **VEGAN**

PREP TIME: 10 minutes ◇ **COOK TIME:** 45 minutes ◇ **SERVES 4**

Chaat are savory, fried snacks enjoyed in many parts of India as street food. They can be made out of so many different ingredients. This recipe is a quick version of one of the popular potato chaat recipes you'll find on the street carts when walking around in Delhi. It features a spice blend called chaat masala, which is a salty-sour mix often sprinkled on top of fresh fruit or used in deep-fried foods to provide an extra edge of flavor. To make this a bit more substantial or even into a light meal instead of a side dish, try adding chickpeas and tomatoes.

1 teaspoon **chaat masala** (see page 7)

¼ teaspoon **red chili powder**

½ teaspoon **ground cumin**

Salt

Canola oil, for deep-frying

6 medium **Yukon Gold potatoes,** peeled and cut into bite-size pieces

2 tablespoons **fresh lime juice** (from 1 or 2 limes)

1. In a small bowl, mix the chaat masala, chili powder, cumin, and salt to taste until well combined.

2. In a deep heavy-bottomed pan or Dutch oven, heat about 3 inches of oil over medium-high heat.

3. Working in batches (do not crowd them in the pan), fry the potatoes in the hot oil for 8 to 10 minutes, until crisp and cooked through. Drain on paper towels.

4. In a large bowl, combine the fried potatoes with the spice mix and toss to coat each piece well. Sprinkle with the lime juice and serve.

GENERAL TIP: You could serve this either as a first course or alongside a meal consisting of a spicy meaty curry, like Keema Masala (page 82).

Moong Salad

◇◇◇◇◇◇◇◇◇◇◇◇◇◇◇◇◇◇◇

DAIRY-FREE ◇ **GLUTEN-FREE** ◇ **VEGAN**

PREP TIME: 10 minutes, plus overnight to soak ◇ COOK TIME: 25 minutes ◇ SERVES 4

This is a classic tangy salad made with green moong lentils, usually served as an evening snack. Moong lentils, also known as mung beans, are native to India. Street vendors in India usually have bowlfuls of hot chopped green chiles from which they take tablespoonfuls and liberally add it to the moong according to the customer's direction. This dish is packed with fiber, protein, iron, and numerous other vitamins and minerals, so it makes an excellent and filling choice for a snack.

1 cup **dried mung beans,** soaked overnight

1 large **Roma tomato,** finely chopped

½ teaspoon **chaat masala** (see page 7)

½ teaspoon **ground cumin**

Salt

Ground black pepper

2 tablespoons **fresh lime juice** (from 1 or 2 limes)

1. Rinse the soaked mung beans thoroughly. Bring a pot of water to a boil over high heat. Add the mung beans and cook for 20 to 25 minutes, until they are al dente. Drain the beans.

2. In a large bowl, combine the cooked mung beans, tomato, chaat masala, cumin, and salt and pepper to taste and mix well. Sprinkle with fresh lime juice and serve.

FLAVOR BOOST: Add finely chopped fresh green chiles to this recipe to give it a stronger kick. If you're looking to turn up the heat but don't want to set your palate on fire, try using fresh green jalapeños, which are a touch milder than other green chiles.

Puris
Deep-Fried Indian Puffy Breads

DAIRY-FREE ◇ **VEGAN**

PREP TIME: 10 minutes, plus 10 minutes to rest ◇ **COOK TIME:** 45 minutes ◇ **SERVES 4**

Puris are traditionally a brunch item, but are also commonly served on a celebratory menu, and you'll soon taste why. This crowd-pleaser originated in the city of Puri, on the eastern coast of India. They classically accompany potato curry or a chickpea dish called Chana Masala (page 86).

2 cups **atta** (Indian whole wheat flour)

½ teaspoon salt

2 tablespoons canola oil, plus more for deep-frying

¾ cup water, plus more as needed

1. In a large bowl, mix together the flour, salt, and 2 tablespoons of oil to combine well. Add the water a little bit at a time and knead to form a smooth dough. Set it aside to rest for 10 minutes.

2. Divide the dough into 12 equal balls and roll out each ball into a thin round.

3. In a Dutch oven or wok, heat 3 inches of oil over medium-high heat.

4. When the oil is hot, slide in a round of dough. Fry it for 3 to 4 minutes, flipping once, until it puffs up and turns golden on both sides.

5. Place the cooked puri on paper towels to drain. Repeat with the remaining rounds of dough. Serve warm.

GENERAL TIP: If you can't serve the puris immediately after frying each one, place the cooked puris on a large baking sheet in a warm oven to keep them fresh and crisp until ready to serve.

Rotis

Whole Wheat Indian Flatbreads

DAIRY-FREE ◇ **KID FRIENDLY** ◇ **VEGAN**

PREP TIME: 10 minutes, plus 10 minutes to rest ◇ **COOK TIME:** 30 minutes ◇ **SERVES 4**

Rotis are traditional Indian breads made with whole wheat flour and traditionally cooked on a hot iron griddle. Unlike most breads, rotis do not include any yeast, so they can be made relatively quickly. They are a regular feature at Indian dinners, and because they are neutral in flavor and take on the flavors of the dish with which they are served, they pair perfectly with any curry, dal, or spiced vegetable dish.

2 cups **atta** (Indian whole wheat flour), plus more for dusting
¾ cup water, plus more as needed

1. Place the flour in a large bowl. A little at a time, add the water and knead to form a smooth, non-sticky dough. Set it aside to rest for 10 minutes.

2. Divide the dough into 8 equal balls and roll each ball into a 6-inch round, dusting lightly with some flour to avoid them sticking to the surface.

3. Heat a nonstick medium skillet over medium-high heat. Cook each roti for 3 to 4 minutes, flipping once during that time and pressing the sides gently until they balloon up and cook through (see General tip). Once you see brown spots on the roti, that means it is cooked through.

GENERAL TIP: The best roti have air pockets in the middle. To create them, press down on the edges of the cooking roti with a thick cloth to enable the air pockets to fill up and cook through. It takes a bit of practice. Once you've perfected the art of making the perfect ballooned roti, you will never want to dip anything else into your curries.

Aloo Tikki

Crispy Potato Cutlets/Cakes

◇◇◇◇◇◇◇◇◇◇◇◇◇◇◇◇◇◇◇◇◇◇◇◇◇◇

DAIRY-FREE ◇ **GLUTEN-FREE** ◇ **KID FRIENDLY** ◇ **VEGAN**

PREP TIME: 20 minutes ◇ **COOK TIME:** 30 minutes ◇ **SERVES 4**

So many cultures enjoy their own version of potato cakes (Jewish latkes, Korean gamja-jeon), but this Indian version crosses all boundaries. Eat them as vegetarian burgers, or make them slider-size to serve as appetizers. This dish uses amchoor (dried mango) powder, which adds a tangy, sour, fruity bent to the flavor of the potato cakes. These are delicious served with tamarind chutney, Green Chutney (page 111), or even just ketchup.

3 large **Yukon Gold potatoes,** boiled until fork-tender (see Ingredient tip) and peeled

3 tablespoons finely chopped **fresh cilantro**

½ teaspoon **red chili powder**

½ teaspoon **ground cumin**

½ teaspoon **amchoor powder**

Salt

1 cup canola oil, for frying

1. In a large bowl, mash the boiled potatoes. Add the cilantro, chili powder, cumin, amchoor powder, and salt to taste and mash so that the spices are evenly distributed among the potatoes. Divide the spiced potato mixture into 12 to 16 equal portions, depending on the size you prefer. Mold each portion into a round patty.

2. In an 11- or 12-inch nonstick skillet, heat 3 to 4 tablespoons of oil over medium-high heat. Add a few patties at a time so as not to crowd the pan and cook, flipping once, for 2 to 3 minutes per side, until the patties are golden and crisp. Drain on paper towels. Repeat with the remaining patties and more oil. Serve warm.

INGREDIENT TIP: To boil the potatoes, place them in a deep saucepan with water to cover. Bring to a boil and cook until you can easily prick a fork into them without any effort.

Masala Omelet
Indian-Style Spiced Omelet

◇◇◇◇◇◇◇◇◇◇◇◇◇◇◇◇◇◇◇◇◇◇◇◇◇◇◇

30 MINUTES OR LESS ◇ **DAIRY-FREE** ◇ **VEGETARIAN**

PREP TIME: 10 minutes ◇ **COOK TIME:** 5 minutes ◇ **SERVES 1**

The masala omelet is a regular on every breakfast menu in Indian homes. It includes a mix of onions, chiles, and fresh cilantro along with a touch of spicy heat. In an Indian kitchen, an omelet is an opportunity to exhibit the abundance of spices and seasonings; it is often hard for cooks to refrain from adding the numerous options and blends. Here, we keep it simple but delicious. You should feel free to add your own touch. Try serving with Rotis (page 30) or Parathas (page 34)!

2 large **eggs**

1 tablespoon finely chopped **yellow onion**

1 tablespoon finely chopped **Roma tomato**

1 tablespoon finely chopped **fresh cilantro leaves**

Pinch **red chili powder**

Salt

Ground black pepper

1 teaspoon canola oil

1. In a medium bowl, combine the eggs, onion, tomato, cilantro, chili powder, and salt and pepper to taste. Beat vigorously with a fork to mix well.

2. In an 11-or 12-inch nonstick skillet, heat the oil over medium-high heat. Pour in the egg mixture, reduce the heat to medium-low, and cook for 1 to 2 minutes on one side until the egg is set. Flip the omelet over to the other side using a wide spatula and cook for another minute or so, until the omelet is cooked through and firm. Serve warm.

VARIATION: I like to roll this omelet in a warm tortilla and serve it with some tangy chutney to eat for a quick and filling lunch. Or jazz it up with spinach, mushrooms, or even cheese.

Masala Puri
Spiced Deep-Fried Indian Puffy Bread

◇◇◇◇◇◇◇◇◇◇◇◇◇◇◇◇◇◇◇◇◇◇◇◇◇◇◇◇◇◇◇◇◇

DAIRY-FREE ◇ **VEGAN**

PREP TIME: 5 minutes, plus 10 minutes to rest
COOK TIME: 25 to 30 minutes ◇ **SERVES 4**

Masala puri is a street food hailing from Bangalore. Puris are usually served immediately as they are taken out of the oil, super warm and crisp. But sometimes that timing doesn't work with today's schedules, so I usually place the puris on a large baking sheet in a warm oven to keep them fresh and crisp until I'm ready to serve everyone at once.

2 cups **atta** (Indian whole wheat flour)

2 tablespoons canola oil, plus more for frying

1 teaspoon **fennel seeds,** lightly crushed in the palms of your hands

½ teaspoon **red chili powder**

½ teaspoon salt

¼ teaspoon **ground turmeric**

¾ cup water, plus more as needed

1. In a large bowl, mix together the flour, 2 tablespoons of oil, crushed fennel seeds, chili powder, salt, and turmeric to combine well. Add the water, a little bit at a time, and knead it to form a smooth dough. Set it aside to rest for 10 minutes.

2. Divide the dough into 12 equal balls and roll out each ball into a thin round.

3. In a Dutch oven or wok, heat 3 to 4 inches of oil over medium-high heat. Carefully slide one round of dough into the oil and fry for 2 to 3 minutes, until it puffs up and turns golden on both sides. Drain on paper towels. Repeat with the remaining dough rounds. Serve warm.

VARIATION: Replace the fennel seeds with dried mint instead for a fresh twist on the flavor.

Parathas
Fried Indian Flatbreads

DAIRY-FREE ◇ **KID FRIENDLY** ◇ **VEGAN**

PREP TIME: 10 minutes, plus 10 minutes to rest ◇ **COOK TIME:** 30 minutes ◇ **SERVES 4**

Parathas are panfried breads, meaning they are fried in only a small amount of oil, not deep-fried. These are best enjoyed warm, served with a side of chutney or raita. This recipe is the classic version often used as a base for various kinds of stuffing, ranging from meats to vegetables and spices. Aloo parathas, or potato-stuffed parathas, are a classic brunch item served in many Indian homes.

2 cups **atta** (Indian whole wheat flour)
2 tablespoons canola oil, plus more for frying
½ teaspoon salt
¾ cup water, plus more as needed

1. In a large bowl, mix together the flour, 2 tablespoons of oil, and the salt to combine well. Add the water, a little bit at a time, and knead it to form a smooth dough. Set it aside to rest for 10 minutes.

2. Divide the dough into 8 equal balls and roll each ball into a 6-inch round.

3. In a nonstick medium skillet, heat about 1 teaspoon of oil over medium-high heat. Add a dough round to the oil and cook for 3 to 4 minutes, flipping once and adding a few drops of oil to the other side, until it is cooked through and crisp along the edges. You can wrap the parathas in aluminum foil to keep them warm while making the others. Repeat with the remaining oil and dough.

GENERAL TIP: Because these do take some time to prepare, I like to make an extra batch to freeze for later. Wrap the cooked (and cooled) parathas in aluminum foil and place them in freezer bags in the freezer. When you're ready to serve them, thaw completely, and fry them until they have warmed through.

Chana Chaat

Tangy Chickpea Salad

◇◇◇◇◇◇◇◇◇◇◇◇◇◇◇◇◇◇◇◇

30 MINUTES OR LESS ◇ **DAIRY-FREE** ◇ **GLUTEN-FREE**
KID FRIENDLY ◇ **VEGAN**

PREP TIME: 5 minutes, plus 15 minutes to chill ◇ **SERVES 4**

Chaat is actually not one dish but a family of appetizers, small plates, or hors d'oeuvres, similar to tapas in Spain or mezze in Greece. This chickpea chaat is a northern Indian treat commonly purchased from a street hawker and enjoyed as an on-the-go snack. It is a widely popular dish, usually devoured with an extra helping of spicy chutney and fresh green chiles on top. And as snacks go, don't tell the kids, but this is an extra nutritious one.

1 (15-ounce) can **chickpeas,** drained and rinsed thoroughly

2 tablespoons finely chopped **fresh cilantro**

2 tablespoons **fresh lime juice** (from 1 or 2 limes)

½ teaspoon **garam masala,** homemade (page 104) or store-bought

¼ teaspoon **red chili powder**

Salt

In a large bowl, combine the chickpeas, cilantro, lime juice, garam masala, chili powder, and salt to taste. Mix well to combine. Cover and refrigerate for 10 to 15 minutes to allow the flavors to blend. Serve chilled.

VARIATION: For a twist and to make this chaat a bit more substantial, substitute canned mixed beans for the chickpeas and add 1 large chopped Roma tomato. Mix with the spices and lime juice and serve on a bed of fresh crisp lettuce.

Aloo Pakoras

Potato Fritters

◇◇◇◇◇◇◇◇◇◇◇

DAIRY-FREE ◇ **GLUTEN-FREE** ◇ **KID FRIENDLY** ◇ **VEGAN**

PREP TIME: 10 minutes ◇ **COOK TIME:** 45 minutes ◇ **SERVES 4**

This super-popular Indian snack features a crispy outside with a tender, tasty, mouthwatering, soft potato inside. Served with Green Chutney (page 111), these are truly difficult to resist. And save a few for yourself because you won't be able to keep them out of the kids' (and other guests') hands.

1 cup **besan** (chickpea flour)

½ teaspoon **red chili powder**

½ teaspoon **ground cumin**

¼ teaspoon **chaat masala** (see page 7)

Salt

¾ cup water, plus more as needed

Canola oil, for deep-frying

2 large **Yukon Gold potatoes,** thinly sliced crosswise

1. In a large bowl, combine the besan, chili powder, cumin, chaat masala, and salt to taste. Add enough water, a little bit at a time, to form a thick batter.

2. In a heavy-bottomed pot or Dutch oven, heat 3 to 4 inches of oil over medium-high heat until hot. The oil is hot enough when a bit of batter dropped into the oil sizzles on contact. Then reduce the heat to medium to maintain the heat level.

3. Working in batches (do not crowd the pan), dip each slice of potato into the batter to coat well, then carefully drop it into the hot oil. Deep-fry for 6 to 8 minutes, turning them over to ensure that they turn golden brown on all sides. Once the fritters are golden brown and crisp, remove them and set on paper towels to soak up any excess oil. Serve hot.

VARIATION: Use sweet potatoes instead of yellow potatoes for a completely different flavor. Just make sure to cut them into very thin slices horizontally.

Onion Pakoras
Onion Fritters

◇◇◇◇◇◇◇◇◇◇◇

DAIRY-FREE ◇ **GLUTEN-FREE** ◇ **KID FRIENDLY** ◇ **VEGAN**

PREP TIME: 10 minutes ◇ **COOK TIME:** 30 minutes ◇ **SERVES 4**

Sometimes also called pakodas, these fritters are a popular street food throughout India and South Asia. Deep-fried to perfection, these bite-size savory treats will delight your family and guests alike. A note on cutting onions: To prevent burning tears, chill the onions in the refrigerator for a couple of hours before cutting them; it works more often than not.

2 cups chopped **yellow onions** (from about 3 onions)

1 cup **besan** (chickpea flour)

½ teaspoon **fennel seeds**

½ teaspoon **red chili powder**

¼ teaspoon **chaat masala** (see page 7)

Salt

⅓ cup water, plus more as needed

Canola oil, for deep-frying

1. In a large bowl, combine the onions, besan, fennel seeds, chili powder, chaat masala, and salt to taste and mix to combine well. Add the water, a little at a time, to form a thick, smooth batter. You want the onions, spices, and chickpea flour to be able to come together without being runny.

2. In a heavy-bottomed pot or Dutch oven, heat 3 to 4 inches of oil over medium heat. The oil is hot enough when a bit of batter dropped into the oil sizzles on contact.

3. Working in batches (do not crowd the pan), gently add 1-tablespoon dollops of batter to the hot oil and fry for 6 to 8 minutes, flipping them once, until browned and cooked on both sides. Once the fritters are golden brown and crisp, remove them and set on paper towels to soak up any excess oil. Serve hot.

FLAVOR BOOST: These pakoras are best served with some Green Chutney (page 111) on the side.

Corn Chaat
Spiced Corn Salad

◇◇◇◇◇◇◇◇◇◇◇◇◇◇◇◇

30 MINUTES OR LESS ◇ **DAIRY-FREE** ◇ **GLUTEN-FREE** ◇ **VEGAN**

PREP TIME: 10 minutes ◇ **SERVES 4**

The tanginess of the chaat masala spice blend in this recipe pairs perfectly with the sweetness of the corn. Add some heat and you've kicked the flavor up a couple more notches. This dish is a great accompaniment for grilled chicken or fish, or even better, a big bowl of tortilla chips. You could also serve this as a first course or with a spicy meat curry.

2 cups **frozen corn kernels,** thawed and drained

1 small **yellow onion,** finely chopped

1 **jalapeño,** seeded and finely chopped

2 tablespoons **fresh lime juice** (from 1 or 2 limes)

½ teaspoon **chaat masala** (see page 7)

Salt

Ground black pepper

In a large bowl, combine the corn, onion, jalapeño, lime juice, chaat masala, and salt and pepper to taste and mix to combine well. Serve immediately.

INGREDIENT TIP: If you prefer to use fresh corn, just cook the ears in boiling water for about 10 minutes, until the kernels are soft and tender. When cool enough to handle, slice the kernels off the cobs.

Paneer Tikka

◇◇◇◇◇◇◇◇◇◇◇◇◇◇◇◇◇◇◇◇

30 MINUTES OR LESS ◇ **GLUTEN-FREE** ◇ **KID FRIENDLY** ◇ **VEGETARIAN**

PREP TIME: 5 minutes, plus 20 minutes to marinate
COOK TIME: 5 minutes ◇ **SERVES 4**

Paneer is the universally popular Indian fresh cheese made of curds of whole milk formed when an acid (usually lime juice) is added to it. It is most similar to cottage cheese, mild feta, or Mexican queso fresco. Vegans often substitute tofu for paneer because their textures are similar. This dish is delicious served by itself or with any sides that you like—try it with Green Chutney (page 111)!

1 (13- to 15-ounce) package **paneer,** cut into bite-size cubes

½ cup **plain yogurt**

2 tablespoons **fresh lime juice** (from 1 or 2 limes)

2 tablespoons canola oil

1 tablespoon **tandoori masala,** homemade (page 105) or store-bought

½ teaspoon **chaat masala** (see page 7)

Salt

1. In a large bowl, combine the paneer, yogurt, lime juice, oil, tandoori masala, chaat masala, and salt to taste and mix well. Make sure the pieces of paneer are well coated with the other ingredients. Set aside for 20 minutes to let the flavors absorb.

2. Heat an 11- or 12-inch nonstick skillet over medium heat. Add the paneer pieces and cook for 2 to 3 minutes, until they start to brown along the edges. Serve warm.

SUBSTITUTION TIP: For a vegan alternative, use tofu instead of paneer in this recipe. The cooking time is the same.

VARIATION: If you prefer, you can bake the coated paneer in a preheated 425°F oven. Bake for 20 minutes, turning once halfway.

Bharwaan Baingan (Stuffed Baby Eggplants, page 48)

3
Vegetarian Mains

Aloo Gobi

Potato and Cauliflower Stir-Fry

◇◇◇◇◇◇◇◇◇◇◇◇◇◇◇◇◇◇◇◇◇◇◇◇◇◇◇◇◇◇◇◇

DAIRY-FREE ◇ **GLUTEN-FREE** ◇ **VEGAN**

PREP TIME: 10 minutes ◇ **COOK TIME:** 15 to 20 minutes ◇ **SERVES 4**

Aloo gobi is a very popular vegetarian stir-fry of potatoes and cauliflower, mostly found in North India. It is best in the winter months when cauliflower is in season. The chili powder gives the combo a bit of heat, while the amchoor powder (mango powder) balances it out with a tangy twist. This dish goes extremely well with a side of dal and some plain basmati rice or Rotis (page 30).

3 tablespoons canola oil

1 head **cauliflower,** cut into bite-size florets

1 medium **Yukon Gold potato,** cut into bite-size cubes

1 teaspoon **ground coriander**

½ teaspoon **amchoor powder**

¼ teaspoon **red chili powder**

Salt

1. In an 11- or 12-inch skillet, heat the oil over medium-high heat. Add the cauliflower florets and potatoes and stir-fry for 10 to 12 minutes, until they start to brown and are partially cooked.

2. Add the coriander, amchoor powder, chili powder, and salt to taste and stir to mix everything well. Cover and cook for another 4 to 5 minutes, until the cauliflower and potatoes are completely cooked through. Serve warm.

FLAVOR BOOST: Add 1 cup of thawed frozen chopped carrots and/or peas along with the cauliflower to bump up the textures, colors, and nutritional value of this dish.

INGREDIENT TIP: Ground coriander, used in so many Indian recipes, brings gentle, citrusy, refreshing, earthy tones to a dish. The coriander seeds are first dry-roasted before they are finely ground into a powder.

Paneer Bhurji
Scrambled Paneer

◇◇◇◇◇◇◇◇◇◇◇◇◇◇

30 MINUTES OR LESS ◇ **GLUTEN-FREE** ◇ **VEGETARIAN**

PREP TIME: 10 minutes ◇ **COOK TIME:** 10 minutes ◇ **SERVES 4**

This dish is one of my favorite go-to recipes when I'm in a hurry and need to make something quick and simple for dinner. This Indian cheese scramble is flavored simply but powerfully, with onion, tomato, and spices that make this dish irresistible. It is often served with Parathas (page 34) as a light lunch or brunch and can also be used as a filling for sandwiches.

2 tablespoons canola oil

1 medium **yellow onion,** finely chopped

1 tablespoon **ground coriander**

½ teaspoon **red chili powder**

Salt

1 large **Roma tomato,** finely chopped

1 (13- to 15-ounce) package **paneer** (see General tip), grated

1. In an 11- or 12-inch skillet, heat the oil over medium-high heat. Add the onion and cook for 1 to 2 minutes, until the onion starts to lightly brown. Stir occasionally to keep the onion from burning.

2. Add the coriander, chili powder, and salt to taste and mix well. Slowly add the tomatoes and cook for 3 to 4 minutes, until they start to break down and blend in with the spices.

3. Add the grated paneer, stir to combine, and heat for 2 to 3 minutes to warm through before serving.

GENERAL TIP: Homemade paneer is really quite simple, though a bit time consuming. Here's how to DIY paneer: Bring 2 quarts of whole milk just to a boil. Slowly add 2 to 3 tablespoons of fresh lime juice, just enough so that the milk starts to curdle. Turn off the heat and let it rest for a couple of minutes. Line a large bowl with cheesecloth and carefully pour the contents into the cloth-lined bowl. Bring the ends of the cheesecloth together and tie into a tight knot. Let the cheesecloth hang over the kitchen sink so the whey can drip away. After about 1 hour, when all the liquid has drained out, the paneer will form into a firm ball. Slice this into cubes and use as directed.

Aloo Palak

Potatoes with Spinach

◇◇◇◇◇◇◇◇◇◇◇◇◇◇◇◇◇◇◇◇◇

30 MINUTES OR LESS ◇ **DAIRY-FREE** ◇ **GLUTEN-FREE** ◇ **VEGAN**

PREP TIME: 10 minutes ◇ **COOK TIME:** 15 minutes ◇ **SERVES 4**

Aloo palak simply means potatoes and spinach, and it is a very common stir-fry cooked in northern Indian homes. It's an easy, quick, delectable weeknight meal—and a great way to get the kids to eat their spinach. Serve it with Parathas (page 34) or Rotis (page 30). Any leftovers of this dish can be easily stored in the refrigerator for a day or two. The leftovers also tend to taste much better the next day, since as with most Indian recipes, the flavors have had enough time to permeate the dish.

2 tablespoons canola oil

3 large **garlic cloves,** finely chopped

2 medium **Yukon Gold potatoes,** cut into thin wedges

1 tablespoon **ground coriander**

½ teaspoon **red chili powder**

Salt

8 cups roughly chopped **fresh spinach** (see Ingredient tip)

1. In an 11- or 12-inch skillet, heat the oil over medium-high heat. Add the garlic and cook until it starts to sizzle, about 1 minute. Add the potatoes and stir-fry for 8 to 10 minutes, until they start to brown and cook through.

2. Add the coriander, chili powder, and salt to taste and give it a good mix. Stir in the chopped spinach and cook for another 1 to 2 minutes, until the spinach starts to wilt.

3. Give it another mix and serve warm.

INGREDIENT TIP: If you're pressed for time, use a 10-ounce bag of frozen spinach, thawed and drained.

Masala Baingan
Spiced Eggplant

◇◇◇◇◇◇◇◇◇◇◇◇◇◇◇

30 MINUTES OR LESS ◇ **DAIRY-FREE** ◇ **GLUTEN-FREE** ◇ **VEGAN**

PREP TIME: 10 minutes ◇ **COOK TIME:** 10 minutes ◇ **SERVES 4**

Eggplant is a super-versatile vegetable that can be made to take on pretty much any kind of flavor. Plus eggplant is an excellent source of fiber, B vitamins, and potassium, among many other nutrients. This quick and simple recipe is made by sautéing eggplant with a few basic spices. Make it the star of the show with some rice or Rotis (page 30), or serve it alongside a flavorful pilaf with a light chicken dish like Chicken Curry (page 74) and some salad.

2 tablespoons canola oil

1 tablespoon **minced garlic**

1 teaspoon **panch phoron,** homemade (page 106) or store-bought

2 large **eggplants,** unpeeled and cut into bite-size cubes

1 tablespoon **ground coriander**

½ teaspoon **red chili powder**

Salt

1. In an 11- or 12-inch skillet, heat the oil over medium-high heat. Add the garlic and panch phoron. Once the seeds and garlic start to sizzle and become fragrant, about 1 minute, add the chopped eggplant. Cook, stirring occasionally to keep it from burning, for 5 to 6 minutes, until the eggplant starts to lightly brown along the edges.

2. Add the coriander, red chili powder, and salt to taste and mix well. Cover and cook for another 3 to 4 minutes, until the eggplant is completely cooked through. Serve warm.

INGREDIENT TIP: The eggplant called for is just the regular "globe" eggplant found in supermarkets. You could also try this with smaller rounder ones or even long Japanese eggplants.

Bharwaan Baingan
Stuffed Baby Eggplants

◇◇◇◇◇◇◇◇◇◇◇◇◇◇◇◇◇◇◇◇◇◇◇◇

30 MINUTES OR LESS ◇ **DAIRY-FREE** ◇ **GLUTEN-FREE** ◇ **VEGAN**

PREP TIME: 10 minutes ◇ **COOK TIME:** 10 minutes ◇ **SERVES 4**

So many vegetables can be made to taste even better when stuffed with an array of spices. Vegetables like eggplant, zucchini, and okra work extremely well when cooked this way. Here you'll use baby eggplants, which are purple and 2 to 3 inches long. A delicate blend of spices is stuffed inside the eggplants, giving them flavor all the way through their tender middles.

2 tablespoons **ground coriander**

1 tablespoon **tandoori masala,** homemade (page 105) or store-bought

½ teaspoon **garam masala,** homemade (page 104) or store-bought

Salt

8 **baby eggplants**

2 tablespoons canola oil

1. In a small bowl, mix the coriander, tandoori masala, garam masala, and salt to taste and set aside.

2. Starting at the bottom (blossom end) of each eggplant, cut a cross into the flesh to quarter the eggplant lengthwise, going about three-quarters of the way and stopping about ½ inch from the stem end. You are making a space for the spice mixture, but you want the whole eggplant to hold together. Carefully stuff the space between the quarters with the spice mixture. (See Ingredient tip.)

3. In a Dutch oven or large deep skillet, heat the oil over medium-high heat. Carefully place the stuffed eggplants on their sides in the hot oil and sprinkle any leftover spice mixture on top. Give them a quick stir.

4. Cover, reduce the heat to medium-low, and cook, giving the eggplants a quick stir every couple of minutes so that they brown evenly all over but do not burn. Cook for 8 to 10 minutes, until the eggplants are fork-tender and completely cooked through. Serve warm.

GENERAL TIP: This dish is best when featured as the highlight of the meal. Serve it alongside simple and subtly flavored sides like dal (Dal Tadka, page 88) and rice, and stay away from anything that would compete with the robust flavor of the stuffed eggplants.

INGREDIENT TIP: If you have the time, once the eggplants have been filled with the spice mix, refrigerate them for about 30 minutes. This extra time allows the eggplants to absorb as much flavor from the spices as possible. However, if you're short on time, you can go ahead and cook them as soon as they are filled. They will still taste great.

Masala Bhindi

Spiced Okra

◇◇◇◇◇◇◇◇◇◇

30 MINUTES OR LESS ◇ **DAIRY-FREE** ◇ **GLUTEN-FREE** ◇ **VEGAN**

PREP TIME: 10 minutes ◇ **COOK TIME:** 10 minutes ◇ **SERVES 4**

Bhindi is the Indian name for okra (in Indian restaurants, they are also sometimes called "lady fingers" for the vegetable's shape) and this simple stir-fry is a very popular northern Indian recipe. Okra not only has a fresh taste, but also contains numerous nutrients, vitamins, minerals, fiber, and antioxidants. Here, the okra is stir-fried constantly so that it gets tender and well coated with all the spices and onions. This dish can come together in a pretty short amount of time, and is perfect for busy weeknights. I love to serve this with a quick dal and some rice or Rotis (page 30) on the side. Although crisp fresh okra works best and gives the maximum flavor, you can also opt to use frozen chopped okra to save on the preparation time.

2 tablespoons canola oil

1 teaspoon **cumin seeds**

30 to 35 medium **okra pods,** chopped (see Ingredient tip)

1 tablespoon **ground coriander**

½ teaspoon **red chili powder**

¼ teaspoon **ground turmeric**

Salt

1. In an 11- or 12-inch skillet, heat the oil over medium-high heat. Add the cumin seeds and once the cumin seeds start to sizzle, add the okra. Stir-fry for 5 to 6 minutes, until the okra starts to lightly brown along the edges. Stir occasionally to keep it from burning.

2. Add the coriander, chili powder, turmeric, and salt to taste and mix well. Cover and cook for another 1 to 2 minutes, until the okra is completely cooked through. Serve warm.

INGREDIENT TIP: When cooking with fresh okra, be careful to keep it away from as much moisture as possible, because moisture extracts a gooey substance from it. Use a damp cloth to wipe the okra clean, and make sure your knives are wiped dry while chopping it. Stirring the okra while frying not only keeps it from sticking to the bottom of the pan, but also ensures that the spices are well blended with the okra.

Gajar Matar

Carrots and Peas

◇◇◇◇◇◇◇◇◇◇◇◇◇◇

30 MINUTES OR LESS ◇ **DAIRY-FREE** ◇ **GLUTEN-FREE**
KID FRIENDLY ◇ **VEGAN**

PREP TIME: 10 minutes ◇ **COOK TIME:** 15 minutes ◇ **SERVES 4**

Literally translating to carrots and peas, gajar matar is a popular winter staple on many lunch menus across India. Fresh carrots and frozen peas are lightly sautéed with a blend of simple everyday spices, and pair perfectly with almost anything. Serve it up with some dal and rice for a quick weeknight dinner, or make it the main event and serve with Parathas (page 34) or Puris (page 29). Feel free to make this dish a day or two ahead of time; it stores well.

2 tablespoons canola oil

1 teaspoon **panch phoron,** homemade (page 106) or store-bought

2 cups chopped **carrots**

2 cups **frozen peas,** thawed

1 tablespoon **ground coriander**

¼ teaspoon **red chili powder**

Salt

1. In an 11- or 12-inch skillet, heat the oil over medium-high heat. Add the panch phoron and heat until the seeds start to sizzle. Add the carrots and peas and stir-fry for about 10 minutes, or until the carrots start to soften and cook through.

2. Add the coriander, chili powder, and salt to taste and stir to mix everything well. Cover and cook for another 1 to 2 minutes. Serve warm.

FLAVOR BOOST: To bring in even more nutrients (beta-carotene, vitamins C and K, fiber, potassium, etc.!) and some earthy flavor, add 2 cups of chopped spinach in with the spices.

Patta Gobhi Ki Sabzi

Cabbage Stir-Fry

◇◇◇◇◇◇◇◇◇◇◇◇◇◇

30 MINUTES OR LESS ◇ **DAIRY-FREE** ◇ **GLUTEN-FREE** ◇ **VEGAN**

PREP TIME: 10 minutes ◇ **COOK TIME:** 10 minutes ◇ **SERVES 4**

I remember having a dish quite similar to this for dinner a couple of years ago at one of my friend's homes. The spices were subtle, yet added a nice touch to what could be a very bland vegetable, the cabbage. I had to go home and make it my own. The panch phoron seeds first sautéed in the hot oil gave it just the right crunch. This pairs well with Aloo Tikki (Crispy Potato Cutlets/Cakes, page 31).

2 tablespoons canola oil

1 teaspoon **panch phoron,** homemade (page 106) or store-bought

4 cups chopped **green cabbage** (from 1 large cabbage; see Ingredient tip)

1 tablespoon **ground coriander**

¼ teaspoon **ground turmeric**

¼ teaspoon **garam masala,** homemade (page 104) or store-bought

Salt

Ground black pepper

1. In an 11- or 12-inch skillet, heat the oil over medium heat. Add the panch phoron and heat until the seeds start to sizzle. Add the cabbage, increase the heat to medium-high, and cook, stirring occasionally to keep it from burning, for 3 to 4 minutes, until the cabbage starts to soften slightly.

2. Add the coriander, turmeric, garam masala, and salt and pepper to taste and mix well. Cover and cook for another 1 to 2 minutes, until the cabbage is completely cooked through. Serve warm.

INGREDIENT TIP: You can shred cabbage easily with either a mandoline or the shredding disk of a food processor. If you're pressed for time and can't spare a couple of extra minutes for shredding the cabbage and carrots, you can use store-bought coleslaw mix. I usually keep a bag in my refrigerator for days when I need a quick dinner fix. This enables me to cut down on my overall cooking time and get dinner on the table in a flash.

Gobi Matar

Cauliflower and Peas

◇◇◇◇◇◇◇◇◇◇◇◇◇◇◇◇◇◇◇◇

30 MINUTES OR LESS ◇ **DAIRY-FREE** ◇ **GLUTEN-FREE** ◇ **VEGAN**

PREP TIME: 10 minutes ◇ **COOK TIME:** 15 minutes ◇ **SERVES 4**

Gobi matar, or cauliflower cooked with peas, is a classic favorite in the kitchens of northern India. Simple, quick, healthy, and full of Indian aromatics, this dish works well as a main served with some rice or as a substantial side dish with a lighter protein dish like Keema Cutlets (Chicken Patties, page 68). You can also add 1 cup of chopped fresh carrots along with the cauliflower to bump up the presentation and nutritional value.

2 tablespoons canola oil

1 head *cauliflower,* cut into bite-size florets (see Ingredient tip)

1 teaspoon *ground coriander*

¼ teaspoon *ground turmeric*

¼ teaspoon *red chili powder*

Salt

1 cup *frozen peas,* thawed

1. In an 11- or 12-inch skillet, heat the oil over medium heat, then add the cauliflower florets. Stir-fry the cauliflower for 8 to 10 minutes, until it starts to brown and cook through.

2. Add the coriander, turmeric, chili powder, and salt to taste and give it a stir to mix everything well. Add the peas, cover, and cook for another 3 to 4 minutes to warm them through. Serve warm.

INGREDIENT TIP: When cutting cauliflower into florets, make sure to cut them into pieces of equal size, and make them on the small side to cut down on cooking time.

VARIATION: To make the classic restaurant favorite of Aloo Gobi, cut 2 medium potatoes into small bite-size pieces and fry them along with the cauliflower, following the rest of the recipe as directed. Keep in mind that it may take an extra 10 to 15 minutes to cook the potatoes completely through.

Jeera Aloo

Potatoes with Cumin

◇◇◇◇◇◇◇◇◇◇◇◇◇◇◇◇◇◇

30 MINUTES OR LESS ◇ **DAIRY-FREE** ◇ **GLUTEN-FREE** ◇ **VEGAN**

PREP TIME: 10 minutes ◇ **COOK TIME:** 15 minutes ◇ **SERVES 4**

Potatoes are wonderful to use when you want to experiment with spices because they take on any flavor. This recipe is a perfect example of how a handful of basic spices can create an extraordinary flavor profile. Jeera aloo, or potatoes sautéed with whole cumin seeds, is a home-cooked dish popular all over India. Because potatoes are much loved and are some of the most commonly used vegetables in Indian cuisine, there are many simple home recipes that feature them as the main ingredient. Serve them with Parathas (page 34) and Spiced Tomato Raita (page 109).

2 tablespoons canola oil

1 tablespoon **cumin seeds**

4 medium **Yukon Gold potatoes,** cut into bite-size cubes (see Ingredient tip)

½ teaspoon **red chili powder**

¼ teaspoon **ground turmeric**

Salt

1. In an 11- or 12-inch skillet, heat the oil over medium-high heat. Add the cumin seeds and heat until they begin to sizzle. Add the cubed potatoes and stir-fry for 8 to 10 minutes, until the potatoes start to soften.

2. Sprinkle in the chili powder, turmeric, and salt to taste and mix well to combine. Cover and cook for another 4 to 5 minutes, until the potatoes are fork-tender and completely warmed through.

VARIATION: You can change up this recipe to include fresh cauliflower instead of potatoes. Cut a medium head of cauliflower into bite-size florets and let sit in a bowl of cold water for 15 to 20 minutes. This will help the cauliflower stay fresh and crisp. Follow the recipe as directed, swapping out the potatoes for the cauliflower. Keep in mind that the cauliflower will take about half the cooking time, so follow the test for doneness (fork-tender), not the cooking times, and turn off the heat once the florets reach that stage.

Masala Green Beans

30 MINUTES OR LESS ◇ **DAIRY-FREE** ◇ **GLUTEN-FREE**
KID FRIENDLY ◇ **VEGAN**

PREP TIME: 10 minutes ◇ **COOK TIME:** 10 minutes ◇ **SERVES 4**

This is a simple and quick stir-fry recipe. Using familiar green beans makes this a great recipe for introducing beginners to Indian flavors. Green beans are an excellent source of beta-carotene, vitamin C, fiber, and folate, among other nutrients. My favorite way to serve this is with Chicken Curry (page 74) and Matar Pulao (Pea Pulao, page 97), but you can also serve it up with some dal and plain rice for a quick weeknight dinner. The green beans keep perfectly well when stored properly in the refrigerator, and any leftovers can be enjoyed over the next day or two.

2 tablespoons canola oil

1 teaspoon **cumin seeds**

6 cups cut **green beans,** in ½-inch lengths (about 1½ pounds)

1 tablespoon **ground coriander**

1 teaspoon **amchoor powder**

¼ teaspoon **ground turmeric**

Salt

Ground black pepper

1. In an 11- or 12-inch skillet, heat the oil over medium heat. Add the cumin seeds. Once they start to sizzle, add the chopped green beans and stir-fry for 5 to 6 minutes, until they start to brown along the edges.

2. Add the coriander, amchoor powder, turmeric, and salt and pepper to taste and give it a stir to mix everything well. Cook, covered, for another 1 to 2 minutes. Serve warm.

VARIATION: To increase the nutritional value of this recipe and take it a few steps further, you can also add more vegetables like potatoes, peas, and carrots. If you decide to add potatoes, cut them into small bite-size pieces and fry them for 5 to 6 minutes before adding the beans. The frozen peas should be added in the last 3 to 4 minutes of cooking, whereas chopped fresh carrots can be added at the same time as the beans.

Baingan Bhaja
Fried Eggplant

◇◇◇◇◇◇◇◇◇◇◇

DAIRY-FREE ◇ **GLUTEN-FREE** ◇ **VEGAN**

PREP TIME: 10 minutes ◇ **COOK TIME:** 20 to 30 minutes ◇ **SERVES 4**

This popular Bengali recipe is traditionally served as a treat on special occasions. It is usually made during the Hindu festival season, which includes Diwali and Durga Puja, as part of a lavish celebratory menu that includes many dals and pulaos. But it's actually pretty simple, so you can make it on a Wednesday night for dinner, too!

1 tablespoon *tandoori masala,* homemade (page 105) or store-bought

1 tablespoon *ground coriander*

¼ teaspoon *garam masala,* homemade (page 104) or store-bought

Salt

2 large *eggplants,* cut crosswise into ½-inch-thick rounds (see Ingredient tip)

¼ cup canola oil

1. In a small bowl, mix together the tandoori masala, coriander, garam masala, and salt to taste. Sprinkle the spice mix generously on both sides of the eggplant slices to coat well.

2. In an 11- or 12-inch skillet, heat the oil over medium-high heat. Working in batches (do not crowd the pan), carefully add the spiced eggplant slices and fry for 1 to 2 minutes per side, until lightly golden and crisp on both sides. Serve warm.

INGREDIENT TIP: Once you have sliced the eggplants, soak the pieces in a large bowl of cold water for a couple of minutes to get rid of any bitterness. Letting them soak will also slow down the discoloration of the pieces while you prepare the other ingredients. Pat the eggplant slices dry before sprinkling with the spices.

Baingan Chokha
Roasted Eggplant Mash

◇◇◇◇◇◇◇◇◇◇◇◇◇◇◇◇◇◇

DAIRY-FREE ◇ **GLUTEN-FREE** ◇ **KID FRIENDLY** ◇ **VEGAN**

PREP TIME: 10 minutes, plus 15 minutes to rest ◇ **COOK TIME:** 15 minutes ◇ **SERVES 4**

Baingan chokha is a popular dish from the province of Bihar, in the northern part of India. Roasted eggplant is mixed with fresh vegetables and some distinctly Indian seasonings and mashed, which is a completely different take on the veggie. Eat this as a main dish with some rice or Rotis (page 30) and chutney, serve it with Puris (page 29), or enjoy it as a dip with some crackers.

2 large **eggplants** (see Ingredient tip)

1 teaspoon canola oil

1 small **yellow onion,** finely chopped

2 medium **Roma tomatoes,** finely chopped

1 teaspoon finely minced **fresh ginger**

¼ teaspoon **garam masala,** homemade (page 104) or store-bought

Salt

Ground black pepper

1. Preheat the oven to 450°F. Line a baking sheet with parchment paper.

2. Slice the eggplants in half lengthwise and brush with the oil on all sides. Place them cut-side up on the lined baking sheet.

3. Roast the eggplants for 10 to 15 minutes, until the flesh of the eggplants is completely tender. Set them aside to cool.

4. When the eggplants are cool enough to handle, scoop out the flesh into a large bowl (discard the skins). Mash the eggplant until smooth.

5. Add the onion, tomatoes, ginger, garam masala, and salt and pepper to taste. Give it a good mix to combine. Let sit for 10 to 15 minutes before serving so that the flavors have a chance to blend.

INGREDIENT TIP: The best eggplant to use here are the regular "globe" eggplants found in the supermarket. These larger eggplants have a better proportion of flesh to skin.

Khatta-Meetha Kaddu

Sweet and Sour Pumpkin

30 MINUTES OR LESS ◇ **DAIRY-FREE** ◇ **GLUTEN-FREE** ◇ **VEGAN**

PREP TIME: 10 minutes ◇ **COOK TIME:** 10 minutes ◇ **SERVES 4**

Khatta-meetha kaddu is a traditional Indian dish that originated in Rajasthan and Uttar Pradesh. Usually served in winter, the name translates to sweet and sour pumpkin. My recipe is a twist on the original in that it uses butternut squash when it is in season and a blend of delicate spices. The natural sweetness of the squash elevates this recipe. Plus, butternut squash is extremely fortifying, an excellent source of beta-carotene, B vitamins, and vitamins C and E, among other nutrients.

2 tablespoons canola oil

1 tablespoon finely minced **fresh ginger**

4 cups cubed peeled **butternut squash** (about 1 large squash)

1 tablespoon **ground coriander**

½ teaspoon **red chili powder**

¼ teaspoon **amchoor powder**

Salt

1. In an 11- or 12-inch nonstick skillet, heat the oil over medium heat. Add the ginger and heat until it starts to sizzle and become fragrant. Add the butternut squash, increase the heat to medium-high, cover, and cook, stirring occasionally to keep it from burning, for 8 to 10 minutes, until the squash is partially tender.

2. Add the coriander, chili powder, amchoor powder, and salt to taste and mix well. Cover again and continue to cook for another 5 to 6 minutes, until the butternut squash is fork-tender. Serve warm.

SUBSTITUTION TIP: You can substitute sweet potatoes for the butternut squash in this recipe. The result will be even sweeter.

GENERAL TIP: This dish is best enjoyed when served warm. But if you can't leave this dish to prepare at the last minute, you can also make it a day or two in advance. The dish stores perfectly well in the refrigerator in a tightly sealed container. When you are ready to serve, simply warm it in the microwave.

Matar Paneer

Paneer and Peas

◇◇◇◇◇◇◇◇◇◇◇◇

30 MINUTES OR LESS ◇ **GLUTEN-FREE**
KID FRIENDLY ◇ **VEGETARIAN**

PREP TIME: 15 minutes ◇ **COOK TIME:** 15 minutes ◇ **SERVES 4**

If you've ever been to an Indian restaurant, chances are good that you've spotted matar paneer on the menu. The recipe hails from northern India. Chunks of the mild Indian cheese and peas are simmered in a flavorful tomato-based curry that is enjoyed piping hot with fresh, warm Rotis (page 30). This recipe is a very quick and simple version of the classic. Like with most curries, any leftovers will taste even better the next day since the flavors will have a longer time to blend.

3 tablespoons canola oil

4 medium **Roma tomatoes,** finely chopped

1 tablespoon **tandoori masala,** homemade (page 105) or store-bought

¼ teaspoon **garam masala,** homemade (page 104) or store-bought

Salt

1 (13- to 15-ounce) package **paneer,** cut into bite-size cubes

2 cups **frozen peas,** thawed

1 cup water

1. In a medium saucepan, heat the oil over medium-high heat. Add the tomatoes and cook, stirring occasionally to keep them from burning, for 4 to 5 minutes, until they start to break down.

2. Add the tandoori masala, garam masala, and salt to taste and mix well to combine. Slowly add the paneer cubes, peas, and water and mix well. Cover and cook for 5 to 6 minutes, until the curry starts to boil. Turn off the heat and serve warm.

FLAVOR BOOST: Stir in ½ cup of plain yogurt along with the paneer for a much creamier and richer-textured curry.

GENERAL TIP: I often like to make an extra batch of this recipe to save for a later date. Let the dish cool to room temperature before you store it in an airtight container in the freezer. The paneer freezes really well and the flavors get even more concentrated as they sit for a longer time. When you are ready to serve again, let it thaw overnight in the refrigerator before reheating it in the microwave.

Matar Mushroom
Peas and Mushrooms

◇◇◇◇◇◇◇◇◇◇◇◇◇◇◇◇◇◇

30 MINUTES OR LESS ◇ **DAIRY-FREE** ◇ **GLUTEN-FREE** ◇ **VEGAN**

PREP TIME: 10 minutes ◇ **COOK TIME:** 10 minutes ◇ **SERVES 4**

Mushrooms are a great alternative to meat for most vegetarians since they have a nice meaty texture and can take on hearty flavors. This curry is a wonderful way to treat your guests who may not be able to enjoy a chicken curry. In this healthy dish, the spices really highlight and enhance the flavors of the vegetables. It's a simple curry made from just mushrooms, peas, and a few spices. I prefer using cremini mushrooms because they are compact and have a robust flavor, but you can BYOM (bring your own mushrooms) and give this recipe a new twist.

2 tablespoons canola oil

1 large **yellow onion,** finely chopped

20 to 25 **cremini mushrooms,** quartered (see Ingredient tip)

1 tablespoon **ground coriander**

¼ teaspoon **garam masala,** homemade (page 104) or store-bought

Salt

2 cups **frozen peas,** thawed

1. In an 11- or 12-inch skillet, heat the oil over medium-high heat. Add the onion and cook, stirring occasionally to keep it from burning, for 3 to 4 minutes, until it starts to lightly brown.

2. Add the mushrooms and stir-fry for another 3 to 4 minutes, until they start to brown along the edges.

3. Add the coriander, garam masala, and salt to taste and mix well. Slowly add the peas and stir well to combine. Cover and cook for another 1 to 2 minutes to heat through. Serve warm.

INGREDIENT TIP: You can use white button mushrooms, shiitakes, or portobellos here. For the shiitakes, remove and discard the tough stems first. For any mushrooms, don't rinse or submerge them in water as this tends to make them soggy and ruin the texture. Instead, use a damp paper towel or clean cloth to wipe the mushrooms clean.

Saag
Creamy Spinach with Spices

◇◇◇◇◇◇◇◇◇◇◇◇◇◇◇◇◇◇◇◇◇◇◇

30 MINUTES OR LESS ◇ **DAIRY-FREE** ◇ **GLUTEN-FREE** ◇ **VEGAN**

PREP TIME: 10 minutes ◇ **COOK TIME:** 15 minutes ◇ **SERVES 4**

Saag is a very popular and healthy winter spinach recipe that comes from northern India and is traditionally served with hearty Rotis (page 30). When good-quality spinach is not in season, I like to substitute frozen spinach, which is more economical and works well when you need a pureed form. You can also add chunks of paneer to turn this into Palak Paneer.

2 tablespoons canola oil

1 tablespoon finely minced **garlic**

1 tablespoon **tomato paste**

1 teaspoon **ground coriander**

½ teaspoon **red chili powder**

Salt

3 cups **spinach puree** (see Ingredient tip)

1 cup water

1. In a medium saucepan, heat the oil over medium heat. Add the garlic and cook until it begins to sizzle. Add the tomato paste, coriander, chili powder, and salt to taste and mix well.

2. Slowly add the spinach puree and stir well to combine. Add the water and mix again. Reduce the heat to medium-low, cover, and cook for 8 to 10 minutes, just until the saag comes to a boil. Serve warm.

INGREDIENT TIP: Use 2 (10-ounce) bags of frozen chopped spinach. Thaw the frozen spinach and then blend it to a smooth puree in a blender or food processor. This should give you 3 to 4 cups of spinach puree.

VARIATION: To add chicken to this dish, follow the recipe as directed. Once the spinach starts to come to a boil, add 2 boneless, skinless chicken breasts cut into bite-size pieces and about 1 cup of water. Stir everything to mix well and let it cook, covered, until the chicken is cooked through, 8 to 10 minutes. You can add a bit more water if needed. Once the chicken is completely cooked through, turn off the heat and serve it with freshly made naans and a side salad.

Paneer Tikka Masala

<><><><><><><><><><><><><><><><><><><><><><><><>

GLUTEN-FREE ◇ **KID FRIENDLY** ◇ **VEGETARIAN**

PREP TIME: 10 minutes, plus 10 minutes to marinate
COOK TIME: 15 minutes ◇ **SERVES 4**

This traditional North Indian staple is found on many Indian restaurant menus and is a treat to the senses, from its beautiful color to its creamy texture, robust taste, and irresistible aroma. You can easily substitute chicken for the paneer to make Chicken Tikka Masala instead; just be sure to adjust your cooking time accordingly so that the chicken is cooked through (see the Substitution tip).

1 cup **plain yogurt**

1 (13- to 15-ounce) package **paneer,** cut into bite-size cubes

2 tablespoons **tandoori masala,** homemade (page 105) or store-bought

Salt

Ground black pepper

3 tablespoons canola oil

2 medium **yellow onions,** cut into wedges

2 medium **Roma tomatoes,** cut into wedges

1. In a large bowl, beat the yogurt until it is smooth. Add the paneer cubes, tandoori masala, and salt and pepper to taste. Stir well and set the bowl aside for 10 to 15 minutes at room temperature to marinate.

2. In an 11- or 12-inch skillet, heat the oil over medium-high heat. Add the onions and stir-fry for 2 to 3 minutes, until they start to soften. Add the tomatoes and stir-fry for another 1 to 2 minutes.

3. Add the paneer and marinade and cook, stirring occasionally, for 5 to 6 minutes, until the marinade starts to thicken and dry out. Serve warm.

SUBSTITUTION TIP: To make this with chicken instead of paneer, use 2 large boneless, skinless chicken breasts cut into 1-inch cubes. Add the chicken when you would have added the paneer, but increase the cooking time to 8 to 10 minutes to cook the chicken through.

Aloo Matar
Potatoes and Peas

◇◇◇◇◇◇◇◇◇◇◇◇◇◇

30 MINUTES OR LESS ◇ **DAIRY-FREE** ◇ **GLUTEN-FREE**
KID FRIENDLY ◇ **VEGAN**

PREP TIME: 10 minutes ◇ **COOK TIME:** 15 minutes ◇ **SERVES 4**

Aloo matar is one of those go-to weeknight recipes that Indian cooks rely on when they are short on time and ingredients. It uses pantry staples and yet it tastes like you put in hours of cooking time. Serve this with Keema Cutlets (Chicken Patties, page 68) or with some plain basmati rice and a side salad, such as Kachumber (Indian-Style Chopped Salad, page 107), for a quick, healthy meal.

2 tablespoons canola oil

1 tablespoon finely minced *fresh ginger*

4 medium *Yukon Gold potatoes,* cut into bite-size cubes

2 medium *Roma tomatoes,* finely chopped

2 cups *frozen peas,* thawed

1 tablespoon *ground coriander*

Salt

Ground black pepper

1. In a medium saucepan, heat the oil over medium heat. Add the ginger and heat until it starts to sizzle and becomes fragrant. Add the potatoes and cook, stirring occasionally to keep them from burning, for 5 to 6 minutes, until they start to lightly brown along the edges.

2. Add the tomatoes, peas, coriander, and salt and pepper to taste and mix well. Reduce the heat to medium-low, cover, and cook for 6 to 8 minutes, until the potatoes are fork-tender.

3. Give it a final stir and serve warm.

FLAVOR BOOST: Increase the sweetness of this recipe (and the beta-carotene) by using 4 medium sweet potatoes instead of Yukon Gold. Or use a combination of the two.

VARIATION: Make this with cauliflower instead of potatoes. Cut a medium head of cauliflower into bite-size florets and let sit in a bowl of cold water for 15 to 20 minutes. This will help the cauliflower stay fresh and crisp. Add the cauliflower when you would add the potatoes, but the total cooking time will be about half that for the potatoes, so turn off the heat as soon the florets are tender.

Tandoori Lamb Chops, page 83

4

Poultry, Meat, and Fish

Keema Cutlets
Chicken Patties

◇◇◇◇◇◇◇◇◇◇◇◇

DAIRY-FREE ◇ **GLUTEN-FREE** ◇ **KID FRIENDLY**

PREP TIME: 10 minutes ◇ COOK TIME: 25 to 35 minutes ◇ SERVES 4

These chicken patties are serious crowd-pleasers. You won't be able to keep the platter full. You can serve three patties per person as a lunch or dinner with a large salad on the side. Or serve them as appetizers with Matar Paneer (page 60).

1 pound *ground chicken*

3 medium *Yukon Gold potatoes,* boiled (see Ingredient tip, page 31) and mashed

1 tablespoon *tandoori masala,* homemade (page 105) or store-bought

1 tablespoon *ground coriander*

½ teaspoon *red chili powder*

Salt

Canola oil, for frying

1. In a large bowl, combine the ground chicken, mashed potatoes, tandoori masala, coriander, and red chili powder and season with salt. Mix well. Divide the mixture into 12 equal portions and form each portion into a ½-inch-thick patty.

2. In an 11- or 12-inch nonstick skillet, add enough oil to lightly coat the bottom of the pan and heat over medium-high heat. Working in batches (do not overcrowd the pan), place in the number of patties that fit comfortably. Fry the patties for 2 to 3 minutes on each side, until they are golden and crisp, making sure the chicken is completely cooked through and has an internal temperature of 165°F. Continue with the remaining patties, adding more oil as needed. Serve warm.

GENERAL TIP: Make an extra batch of these patties to save for later. Once you have formed the patties (and before cooking them), spread them on a tray and freeze. Once frozen, put them into a zip-seal freezer bag and store in the freezer. The meat freezes really well and the flavors get even more concentrated as they sit for a longer time. When you are ready to serve, let them thaw overnight in the refrigerator before frying as directed.

Chicken Kebabs

GLUTEN-FREE ◇ **KID FRIENDLY**

PREP TIME: 10 minutes ◇ **COOK TIME:** 25 minutes ◇ **SERVES 4**

Though to many a kebab is meat on a skewer, in India a kebab can be any kind of grilled meat dish. There are a ton of different kinds of kebabs in India and they can come in a whole host of shapes—and not on a stick. This chicken version is a widely popular appetizer often served at parties. But with a few sides and some Rotis (page 30) or Parathas (page 34), you can make them into a filling meal.

3 large **boneless, skinless chicken breasts,** cut into 1-inch cubes

1 cup **plain yogurt,** beaten until smooth

2 tablespoons **fresh lemon juice**

2 tablespoons canola oil

1 tablespoon **tandoori masala,** homemade (page 105) or store-bought

½ teaspoon **red chili powder**

Salt

1. Preheat the oven to 425°F. Line a baking sheet with parchment paper.

2. In a large bowl, combine the chicken cubes, yogurt, lemon juice, oil, tandoori masala, and chili powder and season with salt. Mix well to combine. Place the marinated chicken pieces on the lined baking sheet.

3. Transfer to the oven and roast for 20 to 25 minutes, turning once halfway, until the chicken has an internal temperature of 165°F. Serve warm.

VARIATION: Make an Indian chicken pizza! Cook the chicken as directed, then roughly chop it into smaller pieces. Spread store-bought tomato sauce over a ready-made pizza crust. Layer the sauce with sliced onions, bell peppers, and chopped chicken. Top with shredded mozzarella cheese and bake at 425°F until the cheese melts and gets bubbly.

Pepper Chicken

◇◇◇◇◇◇◇◇◇◇◇◇◇◇◇◇◇◇◇◇◇◇◇◇◇◇

30 MINUTES OR LESS ◇ **DAIRY-FREE** ◇ **GLUTEN-FREE** ◇ **KID FRIENDLY**

PREP TIME: 10 minutes ◇ **COOK TIME:** 15 minutes ◇ **SERVES 4**

This recipe was inspired by a South Indian favorite. It originated in Kerela, where black pepper grows in abundance. It's quick to make, hearty, peppery (obviously), and filling, and will surely keep you coming back for more. I like to make this dish on cold winter nights when the body yearns for something warm and comforting.

2 tablespoons canola oil

1 tablespoon finely chopped *garlic*

1 medium *yellow onion,* thinly sliced

3 large *boneless, skinless chicken breasts,* cut into 1-inch cubes

1 tablespoon ground black pepper

1 tablespoon *ground coriander*

Salt

2 tablespoons *fresh lemon juice*

1. In a medium saucepan, heat the oil over medium-high heat. Add the garlic and heat until it starts to sizzle and become fragrant. Add the onion and cook for 1 to 2 minutes, until the onion starts to soften and lightly brown.

2. Add the chicken and stir-fry for 3 to 4 minutes, until the chicken begins to get some color. Add the black pepper and coriander and season with salt. Give it a stir to mix well with the chicken.

3. Reduce the heat to medium, cover, and cook for another 6 to 8 minutes, until the chicken is completely cooked through and has an internal temperature of 165°F.

4. Squeeze fresh lemon juice over the top and serve warm.

GENERAL TIP: Black pepper is native to the southern part of India, which is why it is the main heat enhancer in so many South Indian delicacies. Note, though, that freshly ground black pepper added in considerable amounts can drastically increase the heat level of a dish. So always taste as you add it to the dish to be sure you do not exceed your heat tolerance level (or the preferences of anyone else dining with you).

Achari Chicken

◇◇◇◇◇◇◇◇◇◇◇◇◇◇◇◇◇◇◇◇◇◇◇◇

DAIRY-FREE ◇ **GLUTEN-FREE**

PREP TIME: 10 minutes ◇ **COOK TIME:** 25 minutes ◇ **SERVES 4**

This chicken dish is very popular in North India and is often served at dinner parties because it's so different from the other chicken dishes typical for weeknight meals. The chicken is seasoned with achari masala—a spice blend usually used to make Indian pickle (see Ingredient tip). The longer the chicken marinates, the better it will taste. Serve this with any dal, like Palak Dal (Lentils with Spinach, page 89), or make a vegan version (see the Substitution tip).

3 large **boneless, skinless chicken breasts,** cut into 1-inch cubes

2 tablespoons **fresh lemon juice**

2 tablespoons canola oil

1 tablespoon **achari masala**

1 tablespoon **ground coriander**

½ teaspoon **red chili powder**

Salt

1. Preheat the oven to 425°F. Line a baking sheet with parchment paper.

2. In a large bowl, combine the chicken pieces, lemon juice, oil, achari masala, coriander, and chili powder and season with salt. Mix well to combine.

3. Arrange the marinated chicken pieces on the lined baking sheet. Transfer to the oven and bake for 20 to 25 minutes, turning once halfway, until the chicken pieces turn brown along the edges and reach an internal temperature of 165°F. Serve warm.

INGREDIENT TIP: Achari masala is a blend of seasonings used to make achar (Indian pickle) and is sometimes sold as pickle masala. As with most seasoning blends, it can vary with the brand (or the cook), but often includes red chiles, fenugreek seeds, mustard seeds, salt, and asafoetida.

SUBSTITUTION TIP: For a vegan version, replace the chicken with chunks of vegetables such as cauliflower, carrots, and potatoes. To ensure quick cooking time, cut the potatoes into bite-size dice. Let the curry simmer for 10 to 15 minutes longer to ensure that the potatoes are tender.

Masala Wings

◇◇◇◇◇◇◇◇◇◇◇◇◇◇◇◇◇◇◇◇◇◇

DAIRY-FREE ◇ **GLUTEN-FREE** ◇ **KID FRIENDLY**

PREP TIME: 10 minutes ◇ **COOK TIME:** 25 minutes ◇ **SERVES 4**

Chicken wings in you-name-it sauce are a worldwide sensation, gracing bar menus the world over. This Indian-inspired take on the crowd-pleaser can really step up your watch-party or tailgating game. To make it even better? Cook the wings on an outdoor grill during the summer months (or during tailgating season, too, if you have a portable grill).

20 *chicken wings*

2 tablespoons *fresh lemon juice*

2 tablespoons canola oil

1 tablespoon *tandoori masala,* homemade (page 105) or store-bought

1 tablespoon *ground coriander*

1 teaspoon *garam masala,* homemade (page 104) or store-bought

Salt

1. Preheat the oven to 425°F. Line a baking sheet with parchment paper.

2. In a large bowl, combine the chicken wings, lemon juice, oil, tandoori masala, coriander, and garam masala and season with salt. Toss well to coat.

3. Arrange the chicken wings on the lined baking sheet. Transfer to the oven and roast for 20 to 25 minutes, turning once halfway, until the chicken crisps along the edges. Serve warm.

SUBSTITUTION TIP: A vegetarian version of chicken wings, you say? It is possible if you don't squabble over semantics (no chicken and no real wing shape). Cauliflower is strong enough to stand up to high heat and bland enough to take on any flavor, so try it as an alternative to the chicken in this recipe.

Chicken Fried Indian-Style

30 MINUTES OR LESS ◇ **DAIRY-FREE** ◇ **GLUTEN-FREE** ◇ **KID FRIENDLY**

PREP TIME: 10 minutes ◇ **COOK TIME:** 20 minutes ◇ **SERVES 4**

This is a simple yet classic recipe for Indian-style fried chicken. The amchoor powder (dried mango powder) along with the coriander, cumin, and garam masala really gives the breading on this fried chicken a unique, and delicious, twist. Serve it with Dal Tadka (Everyday Lentils, page 88) and some plain rice.

1 tablespoon **ground coriander**

1 teaspoon **ground cumin**

1 teaspoon **amchoor powder**

1 teaspoon **garam masala,** homemade (page 104) or store-bought

Salt

8 **chicken drumsticks**

Canola oil, for frying

1. In a large bowl, combine the coriander, cumin, amchoor powder, garam masala, and salt to taste. Mix everything well. Add the chicken drumsticks and turn to coat evenly on all sides with the spice mix.

2. In a heavy-bottomed pot, Dutch oven, or deep skillet (like a chicken fryer), heat about 2 inches of oil over medium-high heat. Carefully add half the seasoned chicken drumsticks. Fry for 8 to 10 minutes, until crisp on all sides and completely cooked through with an internal temperature of 165°F. Repeat with the remaining oil and chicken. Serve warm.

SUBSTITUTION TIP: Bake this chicken instead of frying it for a healthier version. Preheat the oven to 450°F. Coat the drumsticks with the spices as directed. Arrange on a parchment-lined baking sheet and bake for 20 to 25 minutes, turning once halfway, until the internal temperature reads 165°F.

Chicken Curry

◇◇◇◇◇◇◇◇◇◇◇◇◇◇◇◇◇◇◇◇◇

30 MINUTES OR LESS ◇ **GLUTEN-FREE**

PREP TIME: 10 minutes ◇ **COOK TIME:** 15 minutes ◇ **SERVES 4**

Chicken curry and rice is a favorite comfort food for many, so this recipe is great when cooking for a crowd. Using boneless chicken does ensure a quick cooking time, but if you have a few extra minutes to spare, use bone-in chicken pieces (such as drumsticks and thighs) instead. It may take a bit of extra cooking time, but it will give the dish a much richer flavor.

2 tablespoons canola oil

1 medium **yellow onion,** finely chopped

2 medium **Roma tomatoes,** finely chopped

2 tablespoons **chicken curry masala** (see Ingredient tip)

3 large **boneless, skinless chicken breasts,** cut into 1-inch cubes

½ cup **plain yogurt,** beaten until smooth

½ cup water

Salt

1. In a medium saucepan, heat the oil over medium-high heat. Add the onion and cook for 1 to 2 minutes, until it starts to soften and lightly brown. Add the tomatoes and cook for another 2 to 3 minutes, until they start to soften and break down. Add the chicken curry masala and give it a stir to mix well with the tomatoes.

2. Add the chicken pieces, mix well, and cook for 3 to 4 minutes, stirring occasionally, until the meat starts to change color.

3. Reduce the heat to medium, stir in the yogurt and water, and season with salt. Cover and cook for another 6 to 8 minutes, until the chicken is completely cooked through and has an internal temperature of 165°F. Serve warm.

SUBSTITUTION TIP: For a vegetarian curry, substitute chunks of vegetables (like cauliflower, carrots, and potatoes) for the chicken. To maintain a quick cooking time, cut the potatoes and carrots into small dice. Let the curry simmer for 10 to 15 minutes longer to ensure that the potatoes are tender and cooked through.

Fish Masala

◇◇◇◇◇◇◇◇◇◇◇◇◇◇◇◇◇◇

30 MINUTES OR LESS ◇ **DAIRY-FREE** ◇ **GLUTEN-FREE** ◇ **KID FRIENDLY**

PREP TIME: 10 minutes ◇ **COOK TIME:** 10 minutes ◇ **SERVES 4**

I love this recipe for its simplicity and speed. It is a breeze to make and a definite crowd-pleaser. One fish that works perfectly here is tilapia, which is fairly mild and can take on the intense flavors of this dish with ease. Serve it with plain basmati rice and enjoy the full flavors.

2 tablespoons canola oil

1 medium *yellow onion,* thinly sliced

4 (6-ounce) *firm-fleshed white fish fillets,* such as tilapia (see Substitution tip), cut into 1-inch pieces

1 tablespoon *tandoori masala,* homemade (page 105) or store-bought

1 tablespoon *ground coriander*

Salt

2 tablespoons *fresh lemon juice*

1. In a large nonstick skillet, heat the oil over medium-high heat. Add the onion and cook for 1 to 2 minutes, until it begins to lightly brown. Add the fish and cook for 2 to 3 minutes, until the pieces begin to brown a bit.

2. Sprinkle with the tandoori masala and coriander and season with salt. Give it a stir to mix everything well. Stir-fry for another 1 to 2 minutes, until the fish is coated with the spices and cooked through.

3. Sprinkle with the lemon juice and serve warm.

SUBSTITUTION TIP: Instead of tilapia, try this recipe with halibut or red snapper. Avoid stronger-tasting fish like salmon because the robust flavor of the fish will interfere with the richness of the stew.

Adraki Jhinga

Ginger Shrimp

◇◇◇◇◇◇◇◇◇◇◇

30 MINUTES OR LESS ◇ **DAIRY-FREE** ◇ **GLUTEN-FREE**

PREP TIME: 10 minutes ◇ **COOK TIME:** 5 minutes ◇ **SERVES 4**

Although shrimp are really easy and quick to cook, a shrimp dish can still give your guests the sense that you have made something fancy. To really impress, pair this simple dish with an equally simple dal like Dal Tadka (Everyday Lentils, page 88), rice, and a salad like Kachumber (Indian-Style Chopped Salad, page 107).

2 tablespoons canola oil

1 tablespoon finely chopped **fresh ginger**

24 **large peeled and deveined shrimp** (see Ingredient tip)

1 tablespoon **ground coriander**

1 teaspoon **garam masala,** homemade (page 104) or store-bought

Salt

2 tablespoons **fresh lemon juice**

1. In an 11- or 12-inch skillet, heat the oil over medium-high heat. Add the ginger and heat until it starts to sizzle and become fragrant. Add the shrimp and stir-fry for 1 to 2 minutes, until they begin to turn pink.

2. Add the coriander and garam masala and season with salt. Give it a stir to mix well. Stir-fry for another 1 to 2 minutes, until the shrimp are pink and coated with the spices.

3. Sprinkle with the lemon juice and serve warm.

INGREDIENT TIP: If you buy raw shrimp already peeled and deveined, it saves a ton of prep time. Or if you like to make shrimp dishes on the spur of the moment, it's always handy to have a bag of frozen shrimp in the freezer. Shrimp freeze wonderfully and literally take minutes to thaw. Place them in a large bowl of cool water and let them rest for a few minutes until the ice melts and the shrimp come to room temperature.

Masala Jhinga

Spiced Shrimp

◇◇◇◇◇◇◇◇◇◇◇

30 MINUTES OR LESS ◇ **DAIRY-FREE** ◇ **GLUTEN-FREE**

PREP TIME: 10 minutes ◇ **COOK TIME:** 5 minutes ◇ **SERVES 4**

This is a great recipe when you're in a time crunch and want something really quick on a busy weeknight. Shrimp is a go-to when I'm in a rush but still want a wholesome, nutritious main dish. If I haven't had time to go out and buy fresh shrimp, I rely on the bag of frozen shrimp I like to keep in my freezer; it thaws in minutes.

2 tablespoons canola oil

24 **large peeled and deveined shrimp**

1 tablespoon **tandoori masala,** homemade (page 105) or store-bought

1 tablespoon **ground coriander**

1 teaspoon **garam masala,** homemade (page 104) or store-bought

Salt

2 tablespoons **fresh lemon juice**

1. In an 11- or 12-inch skillet, heat the oil over medium-high heat. Add the shrimp and stir-fry for 1 to 2 minutes, until they begin to turn pink.

2. Add the tandoori masala, coriander, and garam masala and season with salt. Give it a stir to mix everything well. Stir-fry for 1 to 2 minutes, until the shrimp turn pink and are coated with the spices.

3. Sprinkle with the lemon juice and serve warm.

FLAVOR BOOST: Make this dish heartier, creamier, and richer by stirring in ½ cup of plain yogurt at the end.

Fried Fish

◇◇◇◇◇◇◇◇◇◇◇◇

30 MINUTES OR LESS ◇ **DAIRY-FREE** ◇ **GLUTEN-FREE**

PREP TIME: 10 minutes ◇ **COOK TIME:** 10 minutes ◇ **SERVES 4**

This is a simple yet classic recipe for Indian-style fried fish. On warm summer afternoons, I love to throw the marinated fish on a hot grill and cook it until the ends slightly char to a rich, deep color. When you're buying fresh fish, it should look firm and smell like the sea (and don't buy it if it doesn't). If using frozen fish, allow it to thaw in the refrigerator for a couple of hours before bringing it to room temperature.

1 tablespoon **ground coriander**

1 teaspoon **ground cumin**

1 teaspoon **amchoor powder**

1 teaspoon **garam masala,** homemade (page 104) or store-bought

Salt

4 (6-ounce) **firm-fleshed white fish fillets,** such as tilapia, sea bass, or cod

¼ cup canola oil

1. In a medium bowl, combine the coriander, cumin, amchoor powder, garam masala, and salt to taste. Add the fish and turn to evenly coat all sides with the spice mix.

2. In an 11- or 12-inch skillet, heat the oil over medium-high heat. If you can fit all the fillets in at once, heat all of the oil. Otherwise work in batches and heat only half the oil to start. Carefully add the coated fish fillets (whatever will fit in the pan) and fry for 2 to 3 minutes on each side, until crisp and golden. If necessary, repeat with the remaining oil and fillets. Serve warm.

INGREDIENT TIP: For the fish, choose either sea bass (medium firm in texture and medium in flavor), tilapia (medium firm in texture but milder and sweeter in flavor) or cod (a more tender texture and a milder flavor).

South Indian–Style Fish Curry

◇◇◇◇◇◇◇◇◇◇◇◇◇◇◇

30 MINUTES OR LESS ◇ **DAIRY-FREE** ◇ **GLUTEN-FREE**

PREP TIME: 10 minutes ◇ **COOK TIME:** 10 minutes ◇ **SERVES 4**

This curry hails from southern India, where coconut and seafood figure prominently in the local cuisine. The spices used are fairly mild to allow the sweet flavors of the coconut milk to shine through. This curry is great eaten with a helping of plain white rice, and can even be thinned a little to be enjoyed as a hearty soup. You can use so many kinds of fish or shellfish in this recipe, ranging from tilapia, trout, and halibut to shrimp, each type of seafood imparting its own delicious flavor.

2 tablespoons canola oil

1 teaspoon **black mustard seeds**

1 medium **yellow onion,** finely chopped

2 tablespoons **fish curry masala** (see Ingredient tip)

1 (14-ounce) can **full-fat coconut milk**

4 (6-ounce) **firm-fleshed white fish fillets,** such as sea bass, tilapia, or cod (see Ingredient tip, page 78), cut into 1-inch pieces

Salt

1. In a medium saucepan, heat the oil over medium-high heat. Add the black mustard seeds and heat until they start to sizzle. Add the onion and cook for 1 to 2 minutes, until it starts to soften and lightly brown.

2. Add the fish curry masala and give it a stir to mix well with the onion. Add the coconut milk and cook for 1 to 2 minutes, until it comes to a simmer.

3. Add the fish pieces, season with salt, and mix well. Reduce the heat to medium, cover, and cook for 3 to 4 minutes, until the curry returns to a boil and the fish turns opaque and flaky. Serve warm.

INGREDIENT TIP: Fish curry masala is a seasoning blend designed specifically, as the name would suggest, for fish curry. As with most curry masalas, there is a wide range of components, though fish curry masalas are generally relatively mild and often include cumin, turmeric, and chili.

Fish Tikka

<><><><><><><><><><><><><><>

30 MINUTES OR LESS ◇ **DAIRY-FREE** ◇ **GLUTEN-FREE**

PREP TIME: 10 minutes ◇ **COOK TIME:** 15 minutes ◇ **SERVES 4**

Tikka dishes are first marinated in a simple but powerful combination of Indian-style seasonings. Because fish can sometimes be on the bland side, this treatment yields delicious and moist results. Though a tikka would traditionally be baked in a tandoor, here we bake it in a hot oven, though it could also be done on an outdoor grill (on a grill topper). If you choose to grill it, make sure you use a firm fish that can stand up to the high heat without falling apart. Serve this with a side of salad and a flavorful pilaf, or with some Mango Chutney (page 112) and naan.

4 (6-ounce) **firm white-fleshed fish fillets,** such as sea bass, tilapia, or cod (see Ingredient tip, page 78), cut into 1-inch pieces

2 tablespoons **fresh lemon juice**

2 tablespoons canola oil

1 tablespoon **tandoori masala,** homemade (page 105) or store-bought

1 tablespoon **ground coriander**

½ teaspoon **red chili powder**

Salt

1. Preheat the oven to 425°F. Line a baking sheet with parchment paper.

2. In a large bowl, combine the fish pieces, lemon juice, oil, tandoori masala, coriander, and chili powder and season with salt. Mix well to combine.

3. Place the seasoned fish pieces on the lined baking sheet. Transfer to the oven and roast for 10 to 15 minutes, turning once halfway, until the fish turns opaque and flaky. Serve warm.

SUBSTITUTION TIP: Feel free to use salmon in this recipe. It will have a more robust, richer taste, but works well with the spices here.

VARIATION: Make a fish tikka sandwich. First, make a yogurt sauce: Whisk together 1 cup of plain yogurt, ¼ teaspoon each of red chili powder, ground cumin, dried mint, and a pinch of salt. Lightly toast thick slices of bread and top with lettuce, tomato slices, and some roasted red peppers. Top with the fish tikka, dollop with the yogurt sauce, and sandwich with another slice of toast. Serve with some extra yogurt sauce on the side.

Fish Cutlets

Fish Cakes

◇◇◇◇◇◇◇◇◇

30 MINUTES OR LESS ◇ **DAIRY-FREE** ◇ **GLUTEN-FREE**

PREP TIME: 10 minutes ◇ **COOK TIME:** 15 minutes ◇ **SERVES 4**

These tuna cakes are a much healthier way to enjoy the goodness of tuna without the addition of mayonnaise. Potatoes are used to bind the ingredients together and add body and texture to the cutlets. The freshness of the cilantro and the spices add a subtle bit of flavor. Although I like using canned tuna for this recipe, you can easily substitute canned crabmeat.

1 (5-ounce) can **water-packed tuna,** drained

3 medium **Yukon Gold potatoes,** boiled (see Ingredient tip, page 31) and mashed

3 tablespoons finely chopped **fresh cilantro**

1 teaspoon **garam masala,** homemade (page 104) or store-bought

1 teaspoon **tandoori masala,** homemade (page 105) or store-bought

Salt

½ cup canola oil, divided, for frying

1. In a large bowl, combine the drained tuna, mashed potatoes, cilantro, garam masala, tandoori masala, and salt to taste. Mix well to combine.

2. Divide the mixture into 12 equal portions, and form each portion into a patty about ½ inch thick.

3. In a large nonstick skillet, heat ¼ cup of oil over medium-high heat. Add half the patties and fry for 3 to 4 minutes, until they are golden and crisp on both sides. Repeat with the remaining patties and oil as needed. Serve warm.

INGREDIENT TIP: Do not use canned tuna packed in oil for this recipe. The oil will interfere with the texture of the cutlets and prevent them from binding well. Always use tuna packed in water, and make sure to drain it well to get rid of any excess moisture.

Keema Masala

◇◇◇◇◇◇◇◇◇◇◇◇◇◇◇◇◇◇◇◇◇◇◇◇◇◇◇◇◇

30 MINUTES OR LESS ◇ **DAIRY-FREE** ◇ **GLUTEN-FREE**

PREP TIME: 10 minutes ◇ **COOK TIME:** 15 minutes ◇ **SERVES 4**

Keema masala is a popular minced meat dish made all across India. Ground lamb or mutton are the most frequently used meats, but in areas where the people do eat cow, ground beef often "grounds" this recipe. Once served to Indian royals and now a mainstay in many Indian home kitchens, this dish hasn't quite found its way into mainstream, fancy Indian restaurants yet, so it might be new to you. This dish is best when served with warm Rotis (page 30) or naan, and can be easily frozen for later use.

2 tablespoons canola oil

1 medium **yellow onion,** finely chopped

2 medium **Roma tomatoes,** finely chopped

1 tablespoon **ground coriander**

1 tablespoon **garam masala,** homemade (page 104) or store-bought

1 pound **ground beef**

Salt

1. In a medium saucepan, heat the oil over medium-high heat. Add the onion and cook for 1 to 2 minutes, until it starts to soften and lightly brown.

2. Add the tomatoes and cook for another 2 to 3 minutes, until they start to soften and break down. Add the coriander and garam masala and give it a stir to mix well with the tomatoes. Add the ground beef, mix well, and cook, stirring occasionally, for 3 to 4 minutes, until the meat starts to change color.

3. Reduce the heat to medium, season with salt, cover, and cook for another 6 to 8 minutes, until the beef is completely cooked through. Serve the dish warm.

SUBSTITUTION TIP: Although ground beef and lamb are most frequently used in this recipe, you can sub in lean ground chicken or turkey for a lighter version. Using chicken or turkey will also reduce the cooking time as they tend to brown and cook through much more quickly.

Tandoori Lamb Chops

◇◇◇

GLUTEN-FREE ◇ **KID FRIENDLY**

PREP TIME: 10 minutes, plus at least 15 minutes to marinate
COOK TIME: 25 minutes ◇ **SERVES 4**

Marinating meat in yogurt is a great way to help tenderize it. In this recipe, lamb chops are coated in a blend of spices and yogurt and set aside for the flavors to penetrate and infuse into the meat. For best results, leave the chops in the marinade overnight in the refrigerator, then let them come to room temperature before cooking. You can make a real upscale meal of this dish by serving it with Jeera Pulao (page 96) and a mildly spiced Cucumber Raita (page 108) for dipping.

12 **lamb rib chops**

1 cup **plain yogurt,** beaten until smooth

2 tablespoons **fresh lemon juice**

2 tablespoons canola oil

1 tablespoon **tandoori masala,** homemade (page 105) or store-bought

½ teaspoon **red chili powder**

Salt

1. In a large bowl, combine the lamb chops, yogurt, lemon juice, oil, tandoori masala, and chili powder and season with salt. Mix well to combine. Let the chops marinate for at least 15 minutes (or ideally overnight in the refrigerator).

2. Preheat the oven to 425°F. Line a baking sheet with parchment paper. Place the coated lamb chops on the lined baking sheet. Transfer to the oven and roast for 20 to 25 minutes, turning once halfway, until they reach an internal temperature of 145°F.

3. Remove from the oven and let the chops rest for a few minutes to allow the juices to redistribute. This will ensure that the meat is perfectly tender and juicy at every bite. Serve warm.

GENERAL TIP: You can also begin the process a few days in advance by combining the lamb chops with the marinade in a zip-seal freezer bag and storing it in the freezer. Before you're ready to cook, let the marinated meat thaw in the refrigerator for a couple of hours, then follow the cooking instructions.

Matar Pulao (Pea Pulao, page 97)

5
Dals, Legumes, and Rice

Chana Masala
Chickpea Curry

◇◇◇◇◇◇◇◇◇◇◇◇◇

30 MINUTES OR LESS ◇ **DAIRY-FREE** ◇ **GLUTEN-FREE**
KID FRIENDLY ◇ **VEGAN**

PREP TIME: 10 minutes ◇ **COOK TIME:** 15 minutes ◇ **SERVES 4**

In many parts of India, particularly the Punjab region, chana masala is a popular street food served alongside the deep-fried bread called Puris (page 29). This simple, healthy dish of chickpeas cooked in a mild curry is a comfort food in Indian homes. Pair it with a side of rice like Jeera Pulao (Cumin Rice, page 96) and some salad like Kachumber (Indian-Style Chopped Salad, page 107) for a complete, well-balanced meal.

2 tablespoons canola oil

1 medium *yellow onion,* finely chopped

1 tablespoon *chana masala seasoning* (see Ingredient tip)

1 teaspoon *garam masala,* homemade (page 104) or store-bought

Salt

3 medium *Roma tomatoes,* finely chopped

1 (15-ounce) can *chickpeas,* drained and rinsed thoroughly

1 cup water

1. In a medium saucepan, heat the oil over medium-high heat. Add the onion and cook for 1 to 2 minutes, until it starts to soften and lightly brown.

2. Add the chana masala seasoning, garam masala, and salt to taste and give it a stir to mix everything well. Mix in the tomatoes and cook for 3 to 4 minutes, until the tomatoes start to break down and blend well with the spices.

3. Add the chickpeas and water and give it a good mix. Reduce the heat to medium, cover, and cook for another 3 to 4 minutes, until the curry starts to come to a boil. Serve warm.

INGREDIENT TIP: Chana masala seasoning is a blend of spices that usually includes coriander and garam masala, and a tart component, such as amchoor powder (dried green mango).

FLAVOR BOOST: Add finely chopped fresh green chiles (to taste) to give this recipe a bit of (or a lot of) a kick.

Khatte Chana

Tangy Chickpeas

◇◇◇◇◇◇◇◇◇◇◇◇◇

30 MINUTES OR LESS ◇ **DAIRY-FREE** ◇ **GLUTEN-FREE**
KID FRIENDLY ◇ **VEGAN**

PREP TIME: 5 minutes ◇ **COOK TIME:** 5 minutes ◇ **SERVES 4**

This northern Indian–style tangy chickpea curry is flavored with a blend of flavorful and complementary spices called chana masala (see Ingredient tip, page 86). The additional amchoor powder added here gives this dish a lovely tart flavor. Serve this with Rotis (page 30) and/or simple basmati rice.

2 tablespoons canola oil
1 (15-ounce) can **chickpeas,** drained and rinsed thoroughly
1 tablespoon **chana masala seasoning**
1 teaspoon **amchoor powder**
½ teaspoon **red chili powder**
Salt
½ cup water
2 tablespoons **fresh lemon juice**

1. In an 11- or 12-inch skillet, heat the oil over medium-high heat. Add the chickpeas and cook for 1 to 2 minutes, until they start to lightly brown.

2. Add the chana masala seasoning, amchoor powder, red chili powder, and salt to taste and give it a stir to mix everything well. Add the water, reduce the heat to medium, cover, and cook for another 1 to 2 minutes, until it starts to come to a boil.

3. Sprinkle with the lemon juice and serve warm.

INGREDIENT TIP: If you'd like to start with dried chickpeas, soak 1 cup of dried chickpeas overnight in a large bowl filled with room-temperature water. The next morning, drain the chickpeas and rinse them thoroughly. Cook the chickpeas in a large pot of boiling water for 30 to 35 minutes, until tender. Use in the recipe as directed.

Dal Tadka

Everyday Lentils

◇◇◇◇◇◇◇◇◇◇◇◇

DAIRY-FREE ◇ **GLUTEN-FREE** ◇ **VEGAN**

PREP TIME: 10 minutes ◇ **COOK TIME:** 25 minutes ◇ **SERVES 4**

An everyday Indian spread is composed of rice, a few Rotis (page 30), a dal (see General tip), and a vegetable, accompanied by some yogurt, Indian pickle, and a light salad. If you don't feel like tackling the whole meal, dals are best enjoyed with a simple rice dish and a dash of pickle. In many Indian households, a different dal is cooked each day, accompanied by a complementary vegetable.

3 cups water

1 cup *masoor dal* (red lentils)

2 tablespoons canola oil

1 tablespoon *panch phoron,* homemade (page 106) or store-bought

2 medium *Roma tomatoes,* finely chopped

½ teaspoon *red chili powder*

¼ teaspoon *ground turmeric*

Salt

1. In a small pot, bring the water to a boil. Add the lentils and boil for about 20 minutes, or until they are soft and cooked through. Set them aside.

2. In a medium saucepan, heat the oil over medium-high heat. Add the panch phoron and heat until the seeds start to sizzle. Add the tomatoes, chili powder, turmeric, and salt to taste. Cook the tomatoes for 2 to 3 minutes, until they start to soften and break down.

3. Slowly add the cooked lentils and give it a stir. Cover, and cook for another 1 to 2 minutes, just until it starts to come to a boil. Serve warm.

GENERAL TIP: Because a huge chunk of the Indian population is vegetarian, lentils play an important role as one of the proteins in their diets. I make a big pot of dal and freeze a batch for busy nights. Thaw it in the refrigerator before reheating.

VARIATION: If you'd like to increase the heat level of this recipe, add chopped fresh green chiles while the dal is cooking. As the dal boils, the heat from the chiles will release into it and the flavor will intensify as it continues to cook.

Palak Dal
Lentils with Spinach

◇◇◇◇◇◇◇◇◇◇◇◇◇◇◇◇◇◇

DAIRY-FREE ◇ **GLUTEN-FREE** ◇ **VEGAN**

PREP TIME: 10 minutes ◇ **COOK TIME:** 25 minutes ◇ **SERVES 4**

This is a very simple home-style dish of lentils cooked with fresh spinach and is often made when spinach is in season. To take advantage of local, seasonal spinach, I make a big pot of palak dal and freeze it. Like most stews, dal freezes beautifully. Thaw it overnight in the refrigerator and let it come to room temperature before warming it in the microwave.

3 cups water

1 cup *masoor dal* (red lentils)

2 tablespoons canola oil

1 tablespoon *cumin seeds*

3 cups chopped *fresh spinach*

½ teaspoon *red chili powder*

¼ teaspoon *ground turmeric*

Salt

1. In a small pot, bring the water to a boil. Add the lentils and boil for about 20 minutes, or until they are soft and cooked through. Set them aside.

2. In a medium saucepan, heat the oil over medium-high heat. Add the cumin seeds and heat until they start to sizzle. Slowly add the cooked lentils and give it a good mix.

3. Add the spinach, chili powder, turmeric, and salt to taste and stir to mix everything well. Cover and cook for 2 to 3 minutes, just until it starts to come to a boil. Serve warm.

INGREDIENT TIP: When fresh spinach isn't in season, you can use a 10-ounce bag of thawed frozen spinach instead.

Sambhar

South Indian–Style Lentil Curry

◇◇◇◇◇◇◇◇◇◇◇◇◇◇◇◇◇◇◇◇◇◇◇◇◇◇◇◇

DAIRY-FREE ◇ **GLUTEN-FREE** ◇ **VEGAN**

PREP TIME: 10 minutes ◇ **COOK TIME:** 30 minutes ◇ **SERVES 4**

Sambhar is a traditional tangy and spicy lentil soup from South India, made with a variety of seasonal vegetables. Sambhar masala is a blend of spices typically used to make this dish. It often contains tamarind, curry leaf, and asafoetida among other more common Indian spices. Sambhar is often paired with crepes called dosas, or steamed rice cakes called idlis. This dish goes well with rice and Fried Fish (page 78).

3 cups water

1 cup **toor dal** (split yellow lentils; see Substitution tip)

2 tablespoons canola oil

1 tablespoon **black mustard seeds**

1 medium **yellow onion,** finely chopped

2 medium **Roma tomatoes,** finely chopped

1 tablespoon **sambhar masala**

Salt

1. In a large pot, bring the water to a boil. Add the lentils and boil for about 20 minutes, or until they are soft and cooked through. Set them aside.

2. In a medium saucepan, heat the oil over medium-high heat, then add the black mustard seeds. Once the seeds start to sizzle, add the onion and cook for 1 to 2 minutes, until it starts to soften and lightly brown. Add the tomatoes, sambhar masala, and salt to taste and cook for another 1 to 2 minutes, until the tomatoes start to break down and pulp.

3. Slowly add the cooked lentils and stir to mix everything well. Cover and cook the curry for 2 to 3 minutes, until it starts to come to a boil. Remove from the heat and serve warm.

SUBSTITUTION TIP: Yellow lentils may be difficult to find unless you are near an Indian market. If you have trouble finding them, try red or brown ones; just keep in mind that different lentils require different cooking times. The package directions can be a guide.

Rajma

Red Kidney Bean Curry

◇◇◇◇◇◇◇◇◇◇◇◇◇◇◇◇◇

30 MINUTES OR LESS ◇ **DAIRY-FREE** ◇ **GLUTEN-FREE**
KID FRIENDLY ◇ **VEGAN**

PREP TIME: 10 minutes ◇ **COOK TIME:** 15 minutes ◇ **SERVES 4**

This red kidney bean curry is a classic favorite in many homes in northern India and is perfect for a simple, hearty weeknight meal. Kidney beans are some of the best plant-based proteins around. They are high in fiber, folate, iron, potassium, and other vitamins and minerals needed for a healthy diet. So, it's for good reason that this vegan recipe should make it into the weekly rotation.

2 tablespoons canola oil

1 medium *yellow onion,* finely chopped

1 tablespoon *rajma masala* (see Ingredient tip)

1 teaspoon *garam masala,* homemade (page 104) or store-bought

Salt

3 medium *Roma tomatoes,* finely chopped

1 (15-ounce) can *red kidney beans,* drained and rinsed thoroughly

1 cup water

1. In a medium saucepan, heat the oil over medium-high heat. Add the onion and cook for 1 to 2 minutes, until it starts to soften and lightly brown.

2. Add the rajma masala, garam masala, and salt to taste and give it a stir to mix everything well. Mix in the tomatoes and cook for 3 to 4 minutes, until the tomatoes start to break down and blend well with the spices.

3. Add the red kidney beans and water and give it a good mix. Reduce the heat to medium, cover, and cook for another 3 to 4 minutes, until the curry just starts to come to a boil. Serve warm.

INGREDIENT TIP: Rajma masala is a spice blend typically used to season this vegetarian kidney bean dish. It often can include chiles, amchoor, ginger, garam masala, cloves, and nutmeg.

Kali Dal

Creamy Black Lentils

◇◇◇◇◇◇◇◇◇◇◇◇◇◇◇◇◇

DAIRY-FREE ◇ **GLUTEN-FREE** ◇ **VEGAN**

PREP TIME: 15 minutes ◇ **COOK TIME:** 30 minutes ◇ **SERVES 4**

This is a simple home-style black lentil curry. Urad dal, or black lentils, are not to be confused with the black lentils sold as "beluga lentils" in many supermarkets. Your best bet for finding them is either in a very well-stocked international aisle or at Indian and South Asian markets. Urad dal, which are actually closely related to the moong bean, tend to be more flavorful than other varieties of Indian lentils and are the must nutritious of the bunch. For a special and elegant meal, serve this dal with a side of grilled tandoori chicken or Chicken Kebabs (page 69), some Rotis (page 30) or naan, and a flavorful rice, like Masala Pulao (Spiced Rice, page 100).

3 cups water

1 cup **urad dal** (black lentils)

2 tablespoons canola oil

1 medium **yellow onion,** finely chopped

1 teaspoon **garam masala,** homemade (page 104) or store-bought

½ teaspoon **red chili powder**

Salt

3 medium **Roma tomatoes,** finely chopped

1. In a small pot, bring the water to a boil. Add the lentils and boil for about 20 minutes, or until they are soft and cooked through. Set them aside.

2. In a medium saucepan, heat the oil over medium-high heat. Add the onion and cook for 1 to 2 minutes, until it starts to soften and lightly brown.

3. Add the garam masala, chili powder, and salt to taste and mix everything well. Mix in the tomatoes and cook for 3 to 4 minutes, until they start to break down and blend well with the spices.

4. Add the cooked lentils and give everything a good mix. Reduce the heat to medium, cover, and cook for another 4 to 5 minutes, until the lentils just start to come to a boil. Serve warm.

FLAVOR BOOST: If you'd like to increase the heat level of this recipe, you can add chopped fresh green chiles while the dal is cooking. As the dal boils, the heat and flavor will intensify as it continues to cook.

Zucchini Dal

◇◇◇◇◇◇◇◇◇◇◇◇◇◇◇◇◇◇◇◇◇

DAIRY-FREE ◇ **GLUTEN-FREE** ◇ **KID FRIENDLY** ◇ **VEGAN**

PREP TIME: 10 minutes ◇ **COOK TIME:** 25 minutes ◇ **SERVES 4**

This recipe is a simple, healthy dish of lentils cooked with fresh zucchini, and is a great way to get the kids to eat their veggies because they are masked in so many delicious flavors. Serve it with plain basmati rice, Matar Pulao (Pea Pulao, page 97) and Cucumber Raita (page 108) on the side.

3 cups water

1 cup *masoor dal* (red lentils)

2 tablespoons canola oil

1 tablespoon *cumin seeds*

3 cups chopped *zucchini* (about 2 medium zucchini)

½ teaspoon *red chili powder*

¼ teaspoon *ground turmeric*

Salt

1. In a small pot, bring the water to a boil. Add the lentils and boil for about 20 minutes, or until they are soft and cooked through. Set them aside.

2. In a medium saucepan, heat the oil over medium-high heat. Add the cumin seeds and heat until they start to sizzle. Add the zucchini, chili powder, turmeric, and salt to taste and stir to mix everything well. Cook for 2 to 3 minutes, stirring occasionally, until the zucchini starts to brown along the edges.

3. Slowly add the cooked lentils and give it a good mix. Cover and cook for another 1 to 2 minutes, until it just starts to come to a boil. Serve warm.

GENERAL TIP: I like to double or triple this recipe and freeze batches of dal for later. Store the dal in the quantities you are likely to use so you don't have to thaw a giant amount if you're not going to use it all. Simply let the dal thaw overnight in the refrigerator and come to room temperature before warming it in the microwave.

Aloo Chana
Chickpeas with Potatoes

◇◇◇◇◇◇◇◇◇◇◇◇◇◇◇◇◇◇◇◇◇

30 MINUTES OR LESS ◇ **DAIRY-FREE** ◇ **GLUTEN-FREE**
KID FRIENDLY ◇ **VEGAN**

PREP TIME: 10 minutes ◇ **COOK TIME:** 15 minutes ◇ **SERVES 4**

Talk about comfort food. This simple dish of chickpeas and potatoes cooked together in a mild curry is an absolute must for those cold winter evenings when you just crave a warm and cozy meal. Pair it with Puris (page 29), Jeera Pulao (Cumin Rice, page 96), and some salad for a complete meal.

2 tablespoons canola oil

1 medium *yellow onion,* finely chopped

2 medium *Yukon Gold potatoes,* finely chopped

1 tablespoon *chana masala seasoning* (see Ingredient tip, page 86)

Salt

2 medium *Roma tomatoes,* finely chopped

1 (15-ounce) can *chickpeas,* drained and rinsed thoroughly

2 cups water

1. In a medium saucepan, heat the oil over medium-high heat. Add the onion and potatoes and cook for 3 to 4 minutes, until the potatoes start to soften and lightly brown along the edges.

2. Add the chana masala seasoning and salt to taste and give it a stir to mix everything well. Mix in the tomatoes and cook for 1 to 2 minutes, until the tomatoes start to soften.

3. Add the chickpeas and water and give it a good mix. Reduce the heat to medium, cover, and cook for another 5 to 6 minutes, until the curry starts to come to a boil and the potatoes are completely cooked through. Serve warm.

VARIATION: Replace the Yukon Gold potatoes with sweet potatoes for a flavor switch and a nutrient boost.

Coconut Rice

◇◇◇◇◇◇◇◇◇◇◇◇◇◇◇◇◇◇◇◇◇◇

30 MINUTES OR LESS ◇ **DAIRY-FREE** ◇ **GLUTEN-FREE**
KID FRIENDLY ◇ **VEGAN**

PREP TIME: 5 minutes ◇ **COOK TIME:** 20 minutes ◇ **SERVES 4**

In this recipe, basmati rice is cooked in coconut milk and flavored with curry leaves and mustard seeds. The curry leaves add a fragrant touch to the overall flavor of this simple dish. Often, I also throw in a handful of mixed beans or frozen peas and carrots to turn this into a meal. Rice is generally consumed at least once a day in India, so it is no surprise that there are usually leftovers. Store leftovers in the refrigerator for up to two days, and just reheat in the microwave when ready to use them.

1 tablespoon canola oil
1 teaspoon **black mustard seeds**
5 or 6 **fresh curry leaves** (see Ingredient tip)
2 cups canned **coconut milk**
2 cups water
2 cups **basmati rice,** rinsed thoroughly
Salt

1. In a medium saucepan, heat the oil over medium heat. Add the mustard seeds and curry leaves. Once the seeds start to sizzle, carefully add the coconut milk and water. Give it a stir and let it come to a slight boil, about 5 minutes.

2. Add the rice and salt to taste and give it a good mix. Reduce the heat to medium-low, cover, and cook for 10 to 12 minutes, until the liquid has evaporated and the rice is completely cooked through. Serve warm.

INGREDIENT TIP: Curry leaves give a wonderful punch of flavor to this dish. Be careful to not let them turn too dark to avoid burning, otherwise it will leave a bitter aftertaste.

Jeera Pulao
Cumin Rice

◇◇◇◇◇◇◇◇◇

30 MINUTES OR LESS ◇ **DAIRY-FREE** ◇ **GLUTEN-FREE**
KID FRIENDLY ◇ **VEGAN**

PREP TIME: 5 minutes ◇ **COOK TIME:** 20 minutes ◇ **SERVES 4**

This recipe will draw people into the kitchen for its aromas. It is a quick and simple dish of fragrant basmati rice cooked with aromatic toasted cumin seeds. Pilaf (another, maybe more familiar, word for pulao) is a reference to rice dishes that are cooked in a flavorful broth and whole spices—sometimes with the addition of meat, vegetables, or nuts. A simple pilaf, like this recipe, goes well with a heftier curry or lentil dish like Kali Dal (Creamy Black Lentils, page 92).

1 tablespoon canola oil
1 tablespoon **cumin seeds**
4 cups water
2 cups **basmati rice,** rinsed thoroughly
Salt

1. In a medium saucepan, heat the oil over medium heat. Add the cumin seeds and heat until they start to sizzle. Carefully add the water, give it a stir, and let it come to a strong simmer.

2. Add the rice and salt to taste and give it a good mix. Reduce the heat to medium-low, cover, and cook for 10 to 12 minutes, until the liquid has been absorbed and the rice is completely cooked through. Serve warm.

VARIATION: For a bit of interest and added color and nutrients, add 1 cup of thawed frozen mixed vegetables to the rice.

Matar Pulao
Pea Pulao

◇◇◇◇◇◇◇◇

30 MINUTES OR LESS ◇ **DAIRY-FREE** ◇ **GLUTEN-FREE**
KID FRIENDLY ◇ **VEGAN**

PREP TIME: 5 minutes ◇ **COOK TIME:** 20 minutes ◇ **SERVES 4**

In this quick and easy recipe, basmati rice is cooked with peas and fragrant spices. Enjoy it as a side with a curry like Rajma (Red Kidney Bean Curry, page 91) and some raita (Cucumber Raita, page 108, or Spiced Tomato Raita, page 109). This recipe is enjoyed all over the Indian subcontinent and soon you'll see why.

1 tablespoon canola oil
1 teaspoon **cumin seeds**
1 cup **frozen peas,**
  thawed and rinsed
4 cups water
2 cups **basmati rice,**
  rinsed thoroughly
Salt

1. In a medium saucepan, heat the oil over medium heat. Add the cumin seeds and heat until they start to sizzle. Carefully add the peas and water and give it a stir. Let it come to a slight boil, about 5 minutes.

2. Add the rice and salt to taste and give it a good mix. Reduce the heat to medium-low, cover, and cook for 10 to 12 minutes, until the liquid has been absorbed and the rice is completely cooked through. Serve warm.

VARIATION: For a bit of a healthy twist, add carrots, corn, and beans to the mix.

Lemon Rice

◇◇◇◇◇◇◇◇◇◇◇◇◇◇◇◇◇◇

30 MINUTES OR LESS ◇ **DAIRY-FREE** ◇ **GLUTEN-FREE**
KID FRIENDLY ◇ **VEGAN**

PREP TIME: 5 minutes ◇ **COOK TIME:** 20 minutes ◇ **SERVES 4**

This dish comes from South India, specifically, Karnataka, where it has become part of the everyday diet. Traditionally, lemon rice was made with a spice mix called gojju, but here you'll make your own spice mix with mustard seeds, curry leaves, salt, fresh lemon juice, and some turmeric to give it the authentic yellow color.

1 tablespoon canola oil
5 or 6 *fresh curry leaves*
1 teaspoon *black mustard seeds*
¼ teaspoon *ground turmeric*
4 cups water
2 cups *basmati rice,* rinsed thoroughly
Salt
2 tablespoons *fresh lemon juice*

1. In a medium saucepan, heat the oil over medium heat. Add the curry leaves, mustard seeds, and turmeric. Once the seeds start to sizzle, carefully add the water. Give it a stir and let it come to a slight boil, about 5 minutes.

2. Add the rice and salt to taste and give it a good mix. Reduce the heat to medium-low, cover, and cook for 10 to 12 minutes, until the liquid is absorbed and the rice is completely cooked through.

3. Remove from the heat, sprinkle with the lemon juice, and carefully fluff the rice with a fork to mix through. Serve warm.

GENERAL TIP: When working with turmeric be careful, because it has been known to stain countertops. If you do get some on the counter, make a mixture of one part baking soda to one part water, scrub it on the stain, and leave it for 15 minutes before wiping. Lemon juice and white vinegar can help as well.

Tomato Rice

◇◇◇◇◇◇◇◇◇◇◇◇◇◇◇◇◇◇◇◇

30 MINUTES OR LESS ◇ **DAIRY-FREE** ◇ **GLUTEN-FREE** ◇ **VEGAN**

PREP TIME: 5 minutes ◇ **COOK TIME:** 20 minutes ◇ **SERVES 4**

A number of cuisines have tomato rice recipes, but this one is uniquely Indian because of the blend of spices and aromatics. The curry leaves offer a fragrant touch to the overall flavor of this simple dish. It is a very popular recipe from South India, where a wide variety of rice dishes reign at nearly every meal. I love to make this dish in the peak of summer when tomatoes are at their best.

1 tablespoon cooking oil

1 teaspoon **black mustard seeds**

5 or 6 **fresh curry leaves**

2 medium **Roma tomatoes,** finely chopped

¼ teaspoon **red chili powder**

Salt

4 cups water

2 cups **basmati rice,** rinsed thoroughly

1. In a medium saucepan, heat the oil over medium heat. Add the mustard seeds and curry leaves. Once the mustard seeds start to sizzle, add the tomatoes, chili powder, and salt to taste and cook for 1 to 2 minutes, until the tomatoes start to break down. Carefully add the water. Give it a stir and let it come to a slight boil, about 5 minutes.

2. Add the rice and give it a good mix. Reduce the heat to medium-low, cover, and cook for 10 to 12 minutes, until the liquid has been absorbed and the rice is completely cooked through. Serve warm.

VARIATION: You can make this dish heartier and more nutritious by adding 1 can of mixed beans. Rinse the canned beans thoroughly to get rid of any excess salt and preservatives, then set them in a sieve or colander to drain completely. Add the beans along with the tomatoes and cook for 5 to 8 minutes, stirring constantly, to enable the tomatoes to break down and mix well with the beans and spices. Continue the recipe as directed, stirring well to mix all the ingredients evenly.

Masala Pulao
Spiced Rice

◇◇◇◇◇◇◇◇◇

30 MINUTES OR LESS ◇ **DAIRY-FREE** ◇ **GLUTEN-FREE** ◇ **VEGAN**

PREP TIME: 5 minutes ◇ **COOK TIME:** 20 minutes ◇ **SERVES 4**

Often, when I'm pressed for time after a long, busy day, I'll make a meal of this simple rice dish; all I need to go with it is a side salad or raita. This well-rounded pulao checks all the boxes for me. It's done in about 25 minutes and it contains all the warm, comforting spices and flavors of home.

1 tablespoon canola oil

1 teaspoon **cumin seeds**

1 medium **yellow onion,** finely chopped

1 teaspoon **garam masala,** homemade (page 104) or store-bought

¼ teaspoon **red chili powder**

Salt

4 cups water

2 cups **basmati rice,** rinsed thoroughly

1. In a medium saucepan, heat the oil over medium heat. Add the cumin seeds and heat until they start to sizzle. Add the onion, garam masala, chili powder, and salt to taste. Cook for 1 to 2 minutes, until the onion starts to lightly brown. Carefully add the water. Give it a stir and let it come to a slight boil, about 5 minutes.

2. Add the rice and give it a good mix. Reduce the heat to medium-low, cover, and cook for 10 to 12 minutes, until the liquid has been absorbed and the rice is completely cooked through. Serve warm.

GENERAL TIP: You can keep any leftovers of this pilaf in the freezer to save for a later date. To do so, simply portion the rice into tightly sealed freezer-safe containers and pop them in the freezer. When you are ready to serve, let the rice thaw on the counter for a couple of hours, then heat it in the microwave to warm completely through.

Green Chutney, page 111

6
Staples

Garam Masala

◇◇◇◇◇◇◇◇◇◇◇◇◇◇◇◇◇◇◇◇◇◇◇

30 MINUTES OR LESS ◇ **DAIRY-FREE** ◇ **GLUTEN-FREE** ◇ **VEGAN**

PREP TIME: 5 minutes, plus 10 minutes to cool ◇ **COOK TIME:** 5 minutes ◇ **MAKES ¼ CUP**

Garam masala is a robust blend of whole spices ground to a powder. This homemade version of the warming spice blend is perfect to use as a finishing spice in most curries. The color and taste in store-bought garam masala often varies depending on the kinds of spices and amounts used. So, it's great to make your own or try different brands to see what suits your taste.

5 *whole cloves*

5 *whole green cardamom pods* (see Ingredient tip)

2 *bay leaves*

1-inch *cinnamon stick*

1 teaspoon *cumin seeds*

1. In an 11- or 12-inch skillet, dry-roast the cloves, cardamom, bay leaves, cinnamon stick, and cumin seeds over medium heat for 1 to 2 minutes, until they start to get fragrant. Be careful not to let them burn.

2. Let them cool for 8 to 10 minutes, then grind them to a fine powder in a spice grinder (or with a mortar and pestle).

3. Store the blend in a cool, dark place in a jar with a tight-fitting lid. It should stay fresh for 2 to 3 weeks. It will lose its aroma when it is no longer fresh.

INGREDIENT TIP: Green cardamom has a slightly sweet aroma and taste. Although it is a popular spice used to flavor Indian curries, it can commonly be found in Indian desserts as well.

Tandoori Masala

◇◇◇◇◇◇◇◇◇◇◇◇◇◇◇◇◇◇◇◇◇◇◇◇◇◇

30 MINUTES OR LESS ◇ **DAIRY-FREE** ◇ **GLUTEN-FREE** ◇ **VEGAN**

PREP TIME: 5 minutes ◇ **MAKES ¼ CUP**

This spice blend is most commonly used in marinades, when making grilled tikkas and tandoori dishes. It adds a slight tang to dishes like Paneer Tikka (page 40) and Bharwaan Baingan (Stuffed Baby Eggplants, page 48). Making your own allows you to adjust the flavor to your liking.

3 tablespoons **ground coriander**

1 tablespoon **amchoor powder**

1 teaspoon **red chili powder**

1 teaspoon **garam masala,** homemade (page 104) or store-bought

1 teaspoon **chaat masala** (see page 7)

1. In a small bowl, mix together the coriander, amchoor powder, chili powder, garam masala, and chaat masala.

2. Store the blend in a cool, dark place in a jar with a tight-fitting lid. It should stay fresh for 2 to 3 weeks. It will lose its aroma when it is no longer fresh.

GENERAL TIP: Most spice blends vary in taste depending on the amount of the individual spices used. Almost every authentic Indian kitchen has its own secret recipe blends. But you can find a good many of the spice blends at most general grocery stores, and pretty much anything you need online (see Resources, page 116).

Panch Phoron

◇◇◇◇◇◇◇◇◇◇◇◇◇◇◇◇◇◇◇◇◇◇◇◇◇

30 MINUTES OR LESS ◇ **DAIRY-FREE** ◇ **GLUTEN-FREE**

PREP TIME: 5 minutes ◇ **MAKES ¼ CUP**

This is a traditional Bengali blend of whole spices, which adds a nice depth of flavor when used in dal or curry recipes. It comprises equal amounts of five different seeds, so is simple to make once you gather all the ingredients. Masala Baingan (Spiced Eggplant, page 47) truly highlights the complex flavors of this authentic Indian five-spice blend.

1 tablespoon
  cumin seeds
1 tablespoon
  fennel seeds
1 tablespoon
  nigella seeds
1 tablespoon
  mustard seeds
1 tablespoon
  fenugreek seeds

1. In a small bowl, mix together the cumin, fennel, nigella, mustard, and fenugreek seeds.

2. Store the blend in a cool, dark place in a jar with a tight-fitting lid. It should stay fresh for 2 to 3 weeks. It will lose its aroma when it is no longer fresh.

GENERAL TIP: Both fenugreek and nigella seeds (potentially the least familiar of the five seeds) can be found at many well-stocked supermarkets. In Indian markets, they are often sold in large packages, which should be stored in a cool, dry place.

Kachumber

Indian-Style Chopped Salad

◇◇◇◇◇◇◇◇◇◇◇◇◇◇◇◇◇◇◇◇◇◇◇◇◇

30 MINUTES OR LESS ◇ **DAIRY-FREE** ◇ **GLUTEN-FREE**
KID FRIENDLY ◇ **VEGAN**

PREP TIME: 10 minutes ◇ **SERVES 4**

This Indian-style salad, reminiscent of similar counterparts in Israel, Greece, and Turkey, commonly includes finely chopped onions, tomatoes, and cucumbers, with a splash of fresh lemon juice. It's quick to make, refreshing to eat, and an excellent and healthy accompaniment to pretty much any dish you're making.

1 cup finely chopped
  cucumber (from 1 large
  English cucumber)
1 cup finely chopped
  tomatoes (from 2 large
  Roma tomatoes)
½ cup finely chopped
  onion (from 1 medium
  yellow onion)
¼ cup finely chopped
  fresh cilantro leaves
¼ cup ***fresh lemon juice***
  (from 2 or 3 lemons)
Salt
Ground black pepper

In a large bowl, combine the cucumber, tomatoes, onion, cilantro, lemon juice, and salt and pepper to taste. Mix all the ingredients together and serve immediately.

INGREDIENT TIP: The range of lemons given for the juice is because some lemons (and limes) contain lots of juice while others contain very little. So get the greater number of lemons/limes to be safe.

Cucumber Raita

<><><><><><><><><><><><><><><><><><><><><><><>

30 MINUTES OR LESS ◇ **GLUTEN-FREE** ◇ **KID FRIENDLY** ◇ **VEGETARIAN**

PREP TIME: 10 minutes ◇ **SERVES 4**

Unlike in North America where yogurt is considered a sweetened, breakfast-y dish, in India it tends toward the savory. A classic use of yogurt at an Indian meal is a raita: a cross between a dip, a condiment, and a salad. Cucumber raita is yogurt stirred together with freshly grated cucumbers and seasoned lightly with spices. Raita helps cool the palate when eating particularly spicy dishes. And yet it stands on its own as an Indian dish, layered and complex in flavor.

2 cups **plain yogurt,** beaten until smooth

¾ cup grated **cucumber** (from 1 cucumber)

1 tablespoon minced **fresh mint leaves**

¼ teaspoon **ground cumin**

¼ teaspoon **red chili powder**

Salt

In a large bowl, combine the yogurt, cucumber, mint, cumin, chili powder, and salt to taste and stir well. Serve immediately.

GENERAL TIP: Raita is best served fresh, just after it is prepared, because it can get a bit watery over time.

Spiced Tomato Raita

30 MINUTES OR LESS ◇ **GLUTEN-FREE**
KID FRIENDLY ◇ **VEGAN**

PREP TIME: 10 minutes ◇ **SERVES 4**

In this raita—a simple homemade way to enhance and cool down many Indian meals—tomatoes add a subtle sweetness to the plain yogurt and give it color and texture. Pair this raita with a meal that consists of a rich curry or dal, like Kali Dal (Creamy Black Lentils, page 92). It also pairs deliciously well with Parathas (page 34).

2 cups *plain yogurt,* beaten until smooth
1 large vine-ripened *tomato,* finely chopped
2 tablespoons minced *fresh cilantro leaves*
¼ teaspoon *ground cumin*
Pinch *red chili powder*
Salt

In a large bowl, combine the yogurt, tomato, cilantro, cumin, chili powder, and salt to taste. Serve immediately.

GENERAL TIP: When mixing the tomato into the yogurt, remember that it will continue to break down and release its juices. So, to avoid the raita thinning down too much, prepare this just when you're ready to serve. If you like your raita a bit chunkier, seed the tomato before adding it.

Instant Chile Achar
Green Chile Pickle

◇◇◇◇◇◇◇◇◇◇◇◇◇◇◇◇

30 MINUTES OR LESS ◇ **DAIRY-FREE** ◇ **GLUTEN-FREE** ◇ **VEGAN**

PREP TIME: 10 minutes ◇ **COOK TIME:** 15 minutes ◇ **MAKES 2 CUPS**

A quick home-style version of the classic green chile pickle is served with most Indian home meals and at many Indian restaurants. This instant pickle is both sweet and sour. The heat level depends on the types of chiles used. Here, I recommend jalapeños, which fall somewhere in the middle of the heat range. To make it spicier, use serrano chiles. This pickle pairs well with any dal or rice.

1 tablespoon canola oil

1 teaspoon **panch phoron,** homemade (page 106) or store-bought

15 large fresh **green jalapeños,** with seeds, cut into ½-inch pieces

1 teaspoon **amchoor powder**

1 teaspoon **sugar**

Salt

1. In a medium nonstick saucepan, heat the oil over medium-high heat. Add the panch phoron and heat until the seeds start to sizzle. Add the jalapeños and stir-fry for about 10 minutes, or until they begin to blister and soften.

2. Stir in the amchoor powder, sugar, and salt to taste. Stir-fry for 1 to 2 minutes, until everything is mixed well.

3. Serve immediately or store in the refrigerator for up to 2 days.

___

GENERAL TIP: You can use any chiles in this recipe. Just choose based on the heat level that you would like the pickle to have in the end.

Green Chutney

◇◇◇◇◇◇◇◇◇◇◇◇◇◇◇◇◇◇◇◇◇◇

**30 MINUTES OR LESS ◇ DAIRY-FREE ◇ GLUTEN-FREE
KID FRIENDLY ◇ VEGAN**

PREP TIME: 10 minutes ◇ **MAKES 1 CUP**

Green chutney stars a winning combination of cilantro and mint and truly highlights the flavors and textures of samosas and Onion Pakoras (page 38). You can also use this chutney as a spread on toast or mixed with warm pasta as a pesto. Because cilantro leaves start to turn dark and brown when kept in extended contact with moisture, this chutney will start to lose its robust green color if kept out for too long. But because it's so quick and easy to make, you can always enjoy this chutney made fresh.

1 cup chopped *fresh cilantro leaves*

½ cup chopped *fresh mint leaves*

2 tablespoons *fresh lemon juice*

1 to 2 tablespoons water

1 *garlic clove,* peeled

¼ teaspoon *ground cumin*

Salt

In a blender or food processor, combine the cilantro, mint, lemon juice, water (more or less to your thickness preference), garlic, cumin, and salt to taste. Blend until smooth. Serve this chutney cool.

GENERAL TIP: Green chutney keeps well in the refrigerator for up to 2 days in an airtight container.

Mango Chutney

◇◇◇◇◇◇◇◇◇◇◇◇◇◇◇◇◇◇◇◇◇◇◇◇◇◇◇◇◇◇◇

30 MINUTES OR LESS ◇ **DAIRY-FREE** ◇ **GLUTEN-FREE**
KID FRIENDLY ◇ **VEGAN**

PREP TIME: 10 minutes ◇ **MAKES 1 CUP**

This is an irresistible sweet and tangy chutney made with fresh mangos and mint. There was a time when I only used this chutney as a dip for finger foods like samosas. Then one day, in a fit of curiosity, I decided to top a scoop of vanilla ice cream with it. I have never looked back.

1 large *ripe mango,* peeled, pitted, and chopped
8 to 10 *fresh mint leaves*
2 tablespoons *fresh lemon juice*
1 tablespoon *sugar*
Salt

In a blender or food processor, combine the mango, mint leaves, lemon juice, sugar, and salt to taste. Blend the ingredients until smooth. Serve immediately.

GENERAL TIP: You can keep any leftovers of this chutney in the refrigerator in an airtight container for 2 to 3 days, but it is best if eaten as soon as it is made. Leftovers can be used to marinate grilled fish or shrimp. You can also thin down this chutney by adding a bit of water, and use it as a salad dressing.

Tomato Chutney

30 MINUTES OR LESS ◇ **DAIRY-FREE** ◇ **GLUTEN-FREE** ◇ **VEGAN**

PREP TIME: 5 minutes ◇ **COOK TIME:** 10 minutes ◇ **MAKES 1 CUP**

I love making a big batch of tomato chutney during the summer months when tomatoes are at peak freshness. I find that fresh, ripe tomatoes, when cooked slowly, release a wonderful sweetness that blends with the spices really well. Refrain from using canned tomatoes to make this chutney. They just don't compare to fresh.

1 tablespoon canola oil

1 teaspoon **black mustard seeds**

3 or 4 **fresh curry leaves**

1 tablespoon minced **garlic**

2 large **Roma tomatoes,** finely chopped

½ teaspoon **red chili powder**

Salt

1. In a nonstick medium saucepan, heat the oil over medium heat. Add the mustard seeds and heat until they start to sizzle. Add the curry leaves and garlic and cook for a few seconds until fragrant.

2. Add the tomatoes and chili powder, reduce the heat to low, and cook until the tomatoes soften and break down, 2 to 3 minutes. Season with salt to taste and serve warm.

GENERAL TIP: This chutney is best if eaten immediately but can be stored in an airtight container in the refrigerator for 2 to 3 days. Warm it before serving.

Measurement Conversions

VOLUME EQUIVALENTS	U.S. STANDARD	U.S. STANDARD (OUNCES)	METRIC (APPROXIMATE)
LIQUID	2 tablespoons	1 fl. oz.	30 mL
	¼ cup	2 fl. oz.	60 mL
	½ cup	4 fl. oz.	120 mL
	1 cup	8 fl. oz.	240 mL
	1½ cups	12 fl. oz.	355 mL
	2 cups or 1 pint	16 fl. oz.	475 mL
	4 cups or 1 quart	32 fl. oz.	1 L
	1 gallon	128 fl. oz.	4 L
DRY	⅛ teaspoon		0.5 mL
	¼ teaspoon		1 mL
	½ teaspoon		2 mL
	¾ teaspoon		4 mL
	1 teaspoon		5 mL
	1 tablespoon		15 mL
	¼ cup		59 mL
	⅓ cup		79 mL
	½ cup		118 mL
	⅔ cup		156 mL
	¾ cup		177 mL
	1 cup		235 mL
	2 cups or 1 pint		475 mL
	3 cups		700 mL
	4 cups or 1 quart		1 L
	½ gallon		2 L
	1 gallon		4 L

OVEN TEMPERATURES

FAHRENHEIT	CELSIUS (APPROXIMATE)
250°F	120°C
300°F	150°C
325°F	165°C
350°F	180°C
375°F	190°C
400°F	200°C
425°F	220°C
450°F	230°C

WEIGHT EQUIVALENTS

U.S. STANDARD	METRIC (APPROXIMATE)
½ ounce	15 g
1 ounce	30 g
2 ounces	60 g
4 ounces	115 g
8 ounces	225 g
12 ounces	340 g
16 ounces or 1 pound	455 g

Resources

Most standard spices and ingredients required for Indian cooking can be found in the international aisle of well-stocked grocery stores and box stores. Here are a few of my favorite brands that you might want to look for:

Eastern

Deep Foods

MDH

MTR

Shan Foods

If you can't find certain ingredients at your local supermarket or Indian grocer, try these online sources:

TheSpicyGourmet.com

DiasporaCo.com

SpiceWallaBrand.com

Arvindas.com

For more easy Indian recipes, you can refer to my blog *Hooked on Heat* (HookedOnHeat.com), as well as my cookbooks:

Knack Indian Cooking

500 Indian Dishes

Instant Pot Vegan Indian Cooking

Index

Acknowledgments

The entire team at Callisto Media, you are all rock stars and this book wouldn't have come to life without you. My family and friends, you always come ready with a spoon to taste anything out of my kitchen—with a smile on your face! And most important, my blog readers, after all these years, you still inspire me to keep cooking.

I thank you all for your love and support. Happy cooking!

Meena Agarwal

(HookedOnHeat.com)

About the Author

 **Meena Agarwal** is a Toronto-based food writer, cooking instructor, and recipe developer. She is the creator of the award-winning food blog, *Hooked on Heat* (HookedOnHeat.com) and author of three previously published cookbooks, *Knack Indian Cooking, 500 Indian Dishes*, and *Instant Pot Vegan Indian Cookbook*. Meena's writing and food reflect the eclectic tastes she has gathered from her Indian and Malaysian heritage, as well as her travels around the globe.

Printed in the USA
CPSIA information can be obtained
at www.ICGtesting.com
LVHW051929091223
765801LV00003B/9